Alien
Nation

Alien Nation

36 True Tales
of Immigration

Edited by Sofija Stefanovic

HARPERVIA

An Imprint of HarperCollins*Publishers*

FIRST EDITION

Illustrations: © Matt Huynh

Designed by SBI Book Arts, LLC

Library of Congress Cataloging-in-Publication Data

Names: Stefanovic, Sofija, editor.
Title: Alien nation : 36 true tales of immigration / edited by Sofija Stefanovic.
Description: First HarperVia hardcover edition. | New York, NY : HarperVia, 2021.
Identifiers: LCCN 2021014843 (print) | LCCN 2021014844 (ebook) | ISBN 9780063062047 (hardcover) | ISBN 9780063062061 (ebook)
Subjects: LCSH: Immigrants—United States—Anecdotes. | Children of immigrants—United States—Anecdotes. | Immigrants—United States—Social conditions. | Children of immigrants—United States—Social conditions. | United States—Emigration and immigration—Social aspects.
Classification: LCC E184.A1 A463 2021 (print) | LCC E184.A1 (ebook) | DDC 305.9/06912073—dc23
LC record available at https://lccn.loc.gov/2021014843
LC ebook record available at https://lccn.loc.gov/2021014844

21 22 23 24 25 LSC 10 9 8 7 6 5 4 3 2 1

Contents

Land Acknowledgment

Most of the pieces in this anthology were performed on Munsee Lenape land. We acknowledge the Lenape people: the first inhabitants and caretakers of the unceded land of present-day New York City. We acknowledge the Lenape people's painful history, honor their ancestors, and pay respects to their past, present, and future.

Several pieces were performed on the traditional lands of the Wurundjeri Woi-wurrung and Boon Wurrung people of the Kulin Nation of present-day Melbourne, Australia. We acknowledge the traditional owners' painful history, and we honor and pay respects to Elders past, present, and future.

Alien
Nation

Introduction

New York City is famously packed with immigrants, with stories that span the world. The Statue of Liberty lives here, holding her torch in welcome. But being new—in New York or any other place—is complicated. Immigrant stories, like the waters Lady Liberty watches, are deep and complex.

Imagine yourself a few miles north of the statue, in Joe's Pub: a plush and cozy space, with cabaret seating and one of the best-known stages in New York City. People sit at little tables drinking cocktails or munching on fries as the lights dim for This Alien Nation, our celebration of immigration.

As host, I usually kick off the evening by fiddling with the mic stand while explaining my accent (the result of traveling back and forth between the former Yugoslavia and Australia as a kid). I introduce the guests, who are here to tell stories of immigration. Each show has a different lineup, and the crowd never knows what they will hear. We could be taken to a wedding in Bangladesh (as told by Abeer Hoque), to an Alexandrian garden half a century ago (courtesy of André Aciman), or a refugee camp in Gaza (recalled by Maysoon Zayid).

For me, our show has always been a balm, a way of feeling less lonely. Guests—some of them well known, others "regular people" (read: fascinating people)—share moments from their lives, reminding us that immigration is not simply a word thrown around in the news (simplified to something you are "for" or "against"), but a world—rich with unique voices, perspectives, and experiences. Immigration is throbbing with talent and potential. My cocreators, Michaela McGuire and Trish Nelson, and I invite guests from New York's diasporas, the literary, comedy, arts, music, and activist worlds.

Our stage at Joe's Pub represents my favorite face of New York: a city of diverse people and stories—stories including the one where Sonia Manzano was honored as "godmother" at the Puerto Rican Day Parade, Tanaïs's olfactory field recording (New York's scent: "turmeric, coconut, tropical fruits, smoke"), Suketu Mehta's brush with the notorious Punjabi Boys Network, or the running jokes of Mazin Sidahmed's Family WhatsApp group. Our talented producer, Shannon Manning, noted that the people watching the show had fascinating stories of their own, so often someone from the crowd gets onstage to share, too. At the end of the show, we leave Joe's Pub having heard something new, our worlds slightly bigger as a result.

One of our regular audience members was the publisher Judith Curr, who was excited to send these stories from the stage into the world. I started putting this anthology together during the lonely year of 2020. For a while, New York City, one of the liveliest places on Earth, became the epicenter of a pandemic. Live shows were canceled. We were alienated from one another. One of my great privileges was listening to recordings from our past shows and compiling the pieces that would go in this book. As I listened, I pretended I was under the warm lights of Joe's Pub, celebrating immigration, surrounded by a lively audience, ice clinking in glasses.

And the pieces were so good! Tatenda Ngwaru recounting her parents trying to protect their intersex child made me cry, as I had hearing it onstage. Xochitl Gonzalez's description of cursed women waiting for a limpia in the Bronx reminded me of the strange and comforting nature of diaspora. The image of Aparna Nancherla's father ordering a pizza in a new land and getting it wrong is as familiar in my mind as if I had been there. These pieces will stay with me forever and offer me comfort and family when I'm feeling alone.

A second joy of putting this book together was contacting our guests again to ask them to adapt their pieces for a reading audience. Despite the vulnerable nature of putting one's life on the page, the contributors rose to the occasion and editing the pieces with them was a delight.

Most of the pieces in this book were first told onstage at Joe's Pub. Several come from This Alien Nation shows we did overseas (Agustinus Wibowo's story was told at Indonesia's Ubud Writers and Readers Festival, and Alice Pung, Maria Tumarkin, and Khalid Warsame performed in Australia, at the Wheeler Centre in Melbourne). A few pieces were written especially for this book, in the hope that they can be performed onstage in the future.

I am honored that our guests have shared their stories. The pieces express the opinions and experiences of their authors, and as you will see, they span comedy and tragedy.

I hope this book thrills and inspires you, no matter where you are from. And I hope it offers community. I imagine people like us—those who have felt alien—reading it and seeing themselves in some of the stories. As a confused immigrant kid who loved books, I wish I'd gotten to read this collection and had seen that there is space in our world for many voices. My kid-self would be delighted to know something she wrote is in this book (though the piece itself—about giving birth—would horrify her).

I've grouped the pieces into show-length segments, curating them as I would our events, in case you want to fix yourself a drink or snack and pretend to be in the audience. Or you can dip into the book any way you like—the pieces stand on their own.

Thank you for joining our celebration of immigration. Please get comfortable and put your hands together for our guests!

—Sofija Stefanovic

1

Alien and Familiar

A teen in 1990s Harlem answers a call from her jailed brother;
a Polish music student seeks adventure in New York;
a disconnected family's WhatsApp group replaces a dinner table;
a Libyan refugee who made it to the US against the odds reflects;
an immigrant mother enrolls her anxious child in Toastmasters

Stories by Cleyvis Natera, Danusia Trevino,
Mazin Sidahmed, Hass Agili, and Aparna Nancherla

The Inheritance of Bone

BY CLEYVIS NATERA

1992

Summer—and with no AC in our Harlem apartment, the days stretched hot and humid and endless and boring because we were supposed to stay put, not hang downstairs during Mami's twelve-hour shifts as a home attendant. Our stepfather had finally gotten a job in a restaurant somewhere far away in Queens. He was gone most of the day, most of the night, and we preferred it that way.

There was only peace when he wasn't there.

That summer, in particular, it felt so good to be free. Our older sister, Shany, had been kicked out and lived with friends in the Bronx, and if Mami was in a good mood, we sometimes got to visit her on weekends. An older stepsister had also been kicked out. We never heard or saw much of her, which was fine by us since she'd always been a snitch. Lindo, our older brother, had gotten locked up, was somewhere upstate. So, out of seven children, only us four youngest kids remained. Me the oldest, at sixteen, and Evelyn, my sister, the youngest at fourteen, with a pair of stepsiblings stair-stepping between us. We'd perfected pancakes, Bundt cakes, donuts. We hung out of the fire escape window, looked through those bars, bopping our heads to the merengue booming out of double-parked cars. We tried to remove the child-locks from the other windows, so we could all hang our heads out but we failed, and instead had to push each other out of the way, to feel whatever breeze happened by, carrying the deliciousness of fried pastelitos being sold out of hot dog carts.

Whenever the phone rang, we listened attentively.

If it was Mami, calling to make sure we were staying put, out of the trouble that lurked outside, the phone rang normally. We snatched it up, knowing that it signaled the freedom to run outside—she only called us once a day. Once downstairs, the three younger kids would rush to the park or the public pool or hang around the block while I stuck close by them, always watchful, always a book under my nose. If it was my brother Lindo calling from prison, the phone rang, paused, then rang for several shorter bursts. That ring we let ring awhile. Or didn't pick up at all.

Truth? It was hard to talk to him. What do you say to your brother in prison?

But on this particular day, after the phone did the Lindo ring, I picked up. It had been several weeks since we spoke. Mami had called around to figure out where he was in the system. But she'd gotten no answers, just "call here, call there," where inevitably, the person with the answers spoke no Spanish.

Now, I accepted the collect call. Lindo greeted me the way he always did.

"Dimelo," he said, in his singsong voice, reserved only

for me. Tell-it-to-me, Tell-me-the-thing, What's-going-on, What's-up, What's-new, What-am-I-missing?

"We're making donuts," I told him, while wondering how to ask him what happened, where he'd been.

"Donuts," he said, wistfully. "Let me hear the street."

I held out the phone for my brother. Out the fire escape there was the sound of an ice cream truck, of police sirens, of children's laughter, of the particular sway and curve of somebody's mom's Dominican Spanish yelled out through space—*HIJODELAGRANPUTAVENPACA*—more moms screamed, more kids ran away, everyone trying to get away from each other, outside confined apartments hot as all hell, looking for air, for breath, for the vibrancy on the outside.

Back in my ear, my brother laughed in reaction to all that noise, "Yo, that sounds like Maria talking so damn loud."

His voice was thick, and I could hear in it the same pain that thickened my voice when I called Papi back in DR, when, at his prompting, I tried to explain what this place was like, all the concrete and bricks under our feet, up the sides of every building.

"You okay?" I said, because I couldn't think of anything else to say.

"Just my feet hurt," he said.

I wanted to call him a liar, to ask why it was so hard for him to just say it hurt, being locked away. But it could be true. My brother and I inherited the bunions that ran on Mami's side of the family. His were more severe than mine—already, at eighteen years old, Lindo's big toe made a sharp curve and crowded the rest of his toes. I grew quiet, looked at my bare feet on the floor. We'd seen it happen to Abuelito, who had terribly deformed feet—his bunions had gotten so bad he hardly wore shoes, even his house slippers had a ripped hole made by the jutted-out bone. Mami wasn't that far behind her father's condition, complaining of sore feet any time she was on her feet for long, which, because of her work, was half a whole day, every day. Back when we all lived together, Lindo and I complained, pissed that Evelyn and Shany had dainty, cute feet, while we inherited bones that would consign us to pain for years to come. Our tia Milagros, who was the only one strong enough to brave bunion surgery, had only gotten one foot done—saying the pain of breaking the bone, then screwing it in place had been far worse than suffering sore feet for life.

"How come you haven't called in so long?" I said.

Lindo explained he'd been placed in solitary, then transferred. He was farther north, no longer in a minimum-security prison as when he'd started his time.

"What the hell did you do this time?" I asked. This, then, the third time he'd been transferred.

"Stand up for myself," he said.

He was quiet for a while. I heard the sounds that surrounded him without him needing to put his phone out: older men's voices. That was it. I imagined the wall of pay phones, how Lindo had no ability to be by himself, to have a private moment. When he first went in, he'd talked nonstop, like a person suffering from a great thirst that could only be satiated by talking without taking a breath. He explained the claustrophobia he felt. To be surrounded by people all the time, even during showers, even on the toilet, supervised, watched over, inspected. Sometimes, he'd said back then, it made him scream. Over the eighteen months he'd been locked away, he shared less and less. This silence had a different texture, a coldness I'd never heard before.

The crime that put him away is only surface, only skin.

For my brother, it didn't start on the corner of 135th Street, with a policeman who saw a seventeen-year-old kid and recognized he'd been arrested before for dealing. It didn't start with him becoming part of a legion representative of years of tough-on-crime policies—a war on drugs that had no impact on drug circulation, but did plenty to lock away kids who looked like us. The hollow? A stepfather who beat Mami one time too many, and on that day, Lindo said fuck it—no more broken nose, no more shattered cheekbones, no more split lip. He stood up for her and ended up sparing Mami a brutal night, but earning himself homelessness. He got kicked out, just like that.

The corner where my brother dealt drugs was just a block away from City College's neo-Gothic campus. Once, during a field trip from my junior high school, we heard that part of those buildings had been made with the bedrock Manhattan stood on. When I'd visited my brother at his corner days later, I had given him that history. He'd looked at me, smirking proudly, and told me that being good at school would pay off for me, he could already tell. "Me, I'm like the bedrock," he said.

I didn't ask him to explain. As a child, up through the time he was sent away, I'd been my brother's shadow, a copy of him that extended beyond his hand-me-downs. My neck always wrinkled looking up to him. Now, I think about how during our first year of school after immigrating from DR, Mami was told by Lindo's eighth-grade teacher he was gifted. He might have used his intelligence in such profound ways. But instead, he'd been bedrock for us, a protector we all needed when he was way too young to even be able to do so—that is, until he was kicked out. And things escalated in terrible ways once he was gone—we were plunged in violence. We were bedrock for him, too, so when he lost his home, and us, he lost his footing. He went from a wild kid who didn't like to listen, to a homeless teen, to a drug dealer within weeks.

After my brother was locked up, any time I walked by those buildings as a teen, I thought about him. Bedrock below the surface, bedrock away from sight, bedrock not good for much, except being stepped on.

Lindo told me on that phone call, his voice with a new coating of steel, that he wasn't a pendejo. He'd learned fast. The one who struck first, who was seen as most brutal, was often left alone, he said. It frightened me to hear him speak like that, to realize that the exact actions he'd tried to prevent in our house were tools for his survival. And in a place where the only solitude that ever existed was freedom from pain, freedom from fear, he'd chosen what it required, never mind what he lost in exchange, hiding himself deeper from the surface until maybe it was difficult for him to figure out where the real him went.

2006

When I was finally able to walk again, I went to my grandparents' house on 144th Street and Broadway. It was Abuelito's birthday, and the family had decided to celebrate it big. Cake, pernil, a bathtub filled with ice and water, beer cooling as it bobbed above the surface—a tiny ocean lapping against the confines of the plastic curtains. The bachata out of giant speakers would leave us all with buzzing eardrums for days to come. Everyone was in a cheerful mood, except me. I hobbled over, each step an aftershock of pain. When I arrived at the couch, I asked for a bendición, getting my kiss on the cheek, and thumped next to Abuelito.

"What have you done to yourself?" he asked in Spanish.

I explained I'd gone through with it—both bunions, at the same time. He stared at me, looked at his feet, torn slippers and all, then puzzled over my bandaged feet, and said, "Why would you cut away your inheritance?"

Mami was there, as were my aunts and uncles, and my dozens of cousins. Everyone laughed. I wasn't sure if it was the painkillers, or the fact I'd been in pain for close to two months with little respite, but I didn't find his statement so funny.

"It was either years of pain in the future with this deformity, or go through this pain now," I said, sharply.

Abuelito placed his arm around me. Then he gently laid both my feet on his lap and patted me carefully on the calf, away from the sore spots. "It was one of the markers in my town, you know. You could recognize who was family by the feet."

There was something so loaded in his tone. Pride, arrogance. But about what?

That day, at my grandparents' house, I thought about my brother, and I thought about the inheritance of bone. I thought about this idea that it was something to be proud of, a life bearing pain. When Lindo was kicked out, no one in our family had offered him a place to live, maybe because he was already seen as a bad seed. We'd all quietly accepted his lot: loneliness, a castaway, a criminal who deserved whatever he got.

By that point, my brother had been living in DR for over a decade. He'd been deported from the third and last prison he'd been transferred to. When I asked him what happened, he'd told me one of the security guards had taken to picking fights with him, bullied him mercilessly in front of his friends. One time, Lindo made to walk away, told this guard over a shoulder that if they'd been outside, it would have been another story. But the guard took off his uniform and flung his weapons. "Let's go," he said, "man to man."

And on a day when my brother should have walked away, he didn't.

Lindo was placed on a flight back to DR. Mami hadn't even found out he was to be deported until he was already gone. Locked out of one country meant locked in another.

When I spoke to Lindo about my intention to do the surgery, he was the only one who said I should do it.

"Cut away the pain right away," he said. "Don't let anyone convince you you gotta live your whole life in fucking pain."

CLEYVIS NATERA is an immigrant from the Dominican Republic, raised in Harlem. She holds a bachelor of arts from Skidmore College and a master's of fine arts in fiction from New York University. She's received awards and fellowships from PEN America, Bread Loaf Writers' Conference, Virginia Center for the Creative Arts, and the *Kenyon Review*'s Summer Workshop, among others. She's published fiction in the *Kenyon Review*, *Aster(ix) Journal*, and *Kweli*. Her nonfiction has been published in *The Washington Post* and most recently anthologized in Marita Golden's *Us Against Alzheimer's*. Her debut novel, *Neruda on the Park*, is forthcoming Spring 2022 from Penguin Random House.

The Scream

BY DANUSIA TREVINO

When I went to say goodbye to my favorite aunt, the night before I was to leave my country, Poland, for good, she placed around my neck—the way medals are given at the Olympics—a necklace made out of ten rolls of toilet paper and said, "Here you go child, show those Americans that we have our own paper to wipe our asses with!"

She didn't know that Americans were not aware (and didn't care) that in 1981 there was a shortage of toilet paper in Poland. In fact, most people used *Pravda*, a Soviet newspaper that means "truth" in Russian, for such needs. It was not an act of political subversion; we did it because *Pravda* was softer and cheaper than our own *Daily News*. I imagine my aunt didn't want me to enter America as yet another poor relative who has nothing to offer except kielbasa. Those rolls of toilet paper were meant to provide me with a sense of worldly confidence and real worth.

I wasn't leaving my country, family, friends, and everything that was dear to me for an abundance of toilet tissue. I was a music student at a university and my violin professor said to me one day: "Cherish these moments. These are the best years of your life." His statement filled me with dread. I wanted more from life than memories, more than to be a music teacher in my hometown.

I certainly was not ready to get married at twenty-one, although me not having a boyfriend yet caused deep concern within my family. I came home one day and was surprised to see my parents in the living room, dressed in their Sunday best on an ordinary Monday. Sitting across from them was a couple and their son. I recognized the father; he was a tombstone maker and had a little shop next to our neighborhood cemetery. The local kids pitied him because he walked with crutches and his body twitched unpredictably. On the coffee table was my mother's favorite Camembert cheese, sliced tomatoes, and a baguette. There was also a bottle of vodka. This had to be a special occasion; Camembert was expensive. They all looked at me, except the son. He was a blond, thin guy of medium height, who was staring at his brown shoes. I immediately smelled a rat. My parents wanted to find a husband for me. The awkwardness of this young man's body reflected what I was feeling inside: a repulsion toward him and myself, for letting this scene go on without protest. After what seemed an eternity, my mom whispered: "Go put something pretty on and come meet this nice young man." I smiled politely and left the room, without saying anything—I never said much. But instead of putting a pretty dress on, I snuck into the basement and climbed up the coal chute toward a tiny window to escape.

I wanted to escape the feeling of insignificance, and of being poor. Although my family never was poor. Nobody lacked basic things in Poland. Education and medical care were free. There was always plenty of work, and I never saw homeless people on the streets. My own family was better off than many others. We had our own land, we grew tomatoes, and we even had our own car. But what we had paled in comparison to the colorful life I saw in French and American movies.

It was while watching Woody Allen's *Manhattan* that I first heard Gershwin's "Rhapsody in Blue," and that music filled me with wildness and yearning for an adventurous and much bigger life. I wanted to learn how to speak English so well that "nobody could tell me nothing." American English, the sounds of which were rounder, thicker, and louder than the language I grew up with. This American English that while learning later would hurt my jaw from stretching it in so many unaccustomed-to-me directions. Polish was beautiful, full of nostalgia and history, but it was dragging my soul down. I wanted to live in America because it was the most powerful country in the world, and I wanted to feel powerful. And it had to be New York City, the coolest of them all. This metropolis that I first met on a page of my geography book when I was nine. The caption underneath the tiny black-and-white photo of a skyscraper read, "New York: a city so tall, that buildings seem to reach the sky, and the traffic is so dense, it's faster to walk than to go in a taxi sometimes." How was that even possible? I could count on my fingers the number of cars in my hometown.

I wanted to be a New Yorker and know the streets as intimately as any good cabdriver does. I wanted to jog in Central Park the way Jill Clayburgh jogged in *An Unmarried Woman*. I wanted to walk in a nonchalant way, the way Americans walk in the world: self-assured, not caring about their wrinkled clothes, unmatched socks, or messy hair. I wanted to get away from the beige elegance of Europe, where bright colors were reserved for children, and on adults were considered cheap and vulgar. I will never forget the time when my school was hosting a choir from California, and we were taking them to the opera. While my friends and I spent days exchanging and borrowing clothes and shoes from others to make sure we looked impressive, the Americans slid into the opera hall with ease, wearing jeans and sneakers. We stood across from them silently, feeling like fools for thinking we could use nice clothes to cover up the shame we felt at not being a part of Western civilization.

I left Poland one month before martial law began. One more month and the trip would have become impossible. My American relatives had no idea that when I asked them for a government-approved invitation to visit their small, suburban house on Long Island, I had bigger plans than to study English for a couple of months. The moment I could say my name and "hello," and understand what HELP WANTED means, I got my first American job.

I still remember the day I got fired from it, barely two weeks after I began. It was at a Burger King in Valley Stream. Apparently, there was something wrong with my burgers. I cried uncontrollably when the manager demanded I give back my brown-and-yellow Burger King uniform. I loved that outfit. We didn't have polyester in Poland, and that uniform represented America to me. As I was sobbing in the bathroom, the cleaning lady—I don't remember what country she was from—wiped away my tears, hugged me, and said, "Don't you worry, honey. You can get a job at Dunkin' Donuts, easily." And as I was about to depart, she added,

"Actually, do something even better for yourself, learn how to type! The future of America is in typing."

I found another job at a factory near my relatives' place to pay for the class and an old electric typing machine to practice on. The classes were at Nassau Community College. The bus was too slow for me to get there on time after work. I went to the first class and asked if anybody lived near me and could give me a ride for the rest of the semester. A young woman with straight, shiny black hair raised her hand and said, "I will pick you up." And for the next few weeks, every Tuesday and Thursday the Italian Anna picked me up in her tiny, cream-colored Renault and drove me to and from class. There was a pink plush dog dangling from her rearview mirror.

One time, while driving on a highway on our way home from school, she suddenly rolled the windows down and—without warning—screamed so loud, as if someone was ripping her skin off without anesthetics. I had never been in the presence of that kind of a sound. Afterward, she smiled apologetically and said, "My parents don't speak any English. I take care of everybody. Things are hard."

"I could never scream like that," I said.

"Well, I will not stop the car until you do."

She passed our exit on the highway.

I kept trying to get the courage by looking at the dangling pink plush dog, but every time Anna counted: "One, two, three—go!" nothing came out of me.

Jumping off the Verrazzano Bridge would have been an easier task to fulfill. After an hour of driving deep into Long Island, I finally let out a scream:

AAAAAAAAAAAAAAAAAAAAAAAAAAHHHHHHH
HHHHHHHHHHHHHHHHHHHHHHHHHHHHHHHH

HHHHHHHHHHHHHHHHHHHHHHHHHHHHHHHHHH HHHHHHH!!!!!!!

Twenty-one years' worth of silence, released onto the Long Island Expressway.

DANUSIA TREVINO is a multidisciplinary artist. Born and raised in Poland, she came to the United States just before martial law began. She received a BFA in photography from NYU. A bass guitarist, Danusia toured the United States and Europe with the NYC punk band FUR. As an actress, she has worked with such notable theater directors as Elizabeth LeCompte (The Wooster Group), Anne Bogart (SITI Company), and Krzysztof Garbaczewski (Dream Adoption Society.) She has performed on numerous stages including the Centre Pompidou in Paris, REDCAT in Los Angeles, the Performing Garage, Skirball Center, and La MaMa in New York. Her films include: *Acts of Worship*, *Where Is Joel Baum?*, *Metamorphosis*, and *Xenophilia*, and she was in the web series *The Louise Log*. A Moth double Grand SLAM winner, Danusia is a regular with Moth Mainstage. Her story "Guilty" has been featured twice on the *Moth Radio Hour*. She was a part of the New York literary salon Women of Letters.

My Family WhatsApp Group

BY MAZIN SIDAHMED

For the past ten years, my family has been scattered all over the world. For a time, my parents and I were in Canada while my sister was in the United Kingdom. Then they were all in Canada, and I was in Sweden. When I got back to Canada, my sister was in Yemen.

Now my parents live in Beirut, the most recent location of my father's work in human rights. We fled Sudan when I was eighteen months old after the recently toppled dictator Omar al-Bashir came into power. First, we lived in the Czech Republic, where my father completed his PhD, before seeking asylum in the UK. My father's career triggered many of the moves since, and my sister and I inherited this restive gene that is wired into people who are forced to leave their homes through no choice of their own. My sister now lives in Brussels, where she does policy work for a humanitarian NGO. I live in New York where I work as a journalist.

Through this all, one thing has kept the four of us connected: our "My Family" WhatsApp group.

The Family WhatsApp group is a modern African tradition.

The app gobbles up most of the phone data on the continent. It works on all devices and allows one to message without using texting credit. Like many families in Sudan and across the continent, my family is huge. My father is one of eleven children and my mother is one of seven, which means I have countless cousins. We're scattered all over Sudan and the planet. WhatsApp lets my auntie in a rural part of Sudan speak with her son in Riyadh with ease. Gone are the days of buying a phone card or going to the internet café once a week to call the family abroad. Our immediate "My Family" WhatsApp group is no different to most I imagine, a healthy mix of updates, photographs, conspiracy theories, and memes—usually of the Mr. Bean variety—my mum's personal fave.

A typical conversation on the WhatsApp group would involve my sister or me asking my parents if they know a Sudanese person that we just met. The answer is usually: "Yes, we are related to them. My cousin-in-law's half brother is their grandfather."

"Thanks, Mum," I'll reply. *Great*, I'll think to myself, *one more person I'll feel guilty for not calling every week.*

My mother is truly the engine of the WhatsApp group. With a flurry of emojis or a dump of twenty-seven blurry photographs of her and my father having dinner, she keeps things alive. Ensuring that no matter how busy my sister and I get in our day-to-day lives, we always remember to check in with "My Family."

My mother is the one asking everybody how they are doing. Pushing for updates and checking on our well-being. For instance, after there was a foiled terrorist attack in Manhattan, my mum quickly turned to the group.

Mum: I just heard about the incident.

Me: I'm fine. I'm in Brooklyn. Very far from the incident.

Mum: [Multiple praying hands emojis] Alhamdulillah. Get out of the USA, it's not safe after Trump's decision on Jerusalem. Please!

Me: Mum, you live in Beirut . . .

Mum: Beirut is now safer than USA.

The hardest thing about being away from my family is our dinner table. We were not the most religious in ensuring that we ate together every evening but when we did, it was usually a joyous occasion. A spirited political debate over postcolonialism could quickly turn to laughter at one of my sister's impersonations. The topic of discussion is usually Sudan or the Middle East. My father, who was a political science professor in Canada, speaks at a snail's pace as he provides historical background on why Egypt and the US work so closely together or whatever it is we're discussing. My mother, an original social justice warrior who studied Russian at university and worked with immigrant women who were victims of domestic violence in the UK, takes a more firebrand approach. My sister and I can quickly end up at loggerheads. Her masterful debating skills often let her wriggle out of any situation, even when she might not know exactly what she's talking about.

Things aren't always so heavy. We've spent many meals listening to my mother make fun of my father about something that happened while they were at university, to which he will break into his kind smile and chuckle while he shakes his head. Or my sister and I will probe them for stories on how they met or our family history.

The "My Family" group is the closest thing I have to the dinner table. The dynamics are much the same. My father is measured and selective with his input, but passionate nonetheless. This usually means not messaging for weeks before sending a long carefully constructed essay with some clearly well-thought-out jokes. I can picture him giddy, smiling to himself as he carefully types it out with one finger, sitting on the couch in his jallabiya. Occasionally, he'll forward a video or something that popped up in another group. "Excerpts from Mandela speeches. If there's one hero for me, it will be him," he sent one day, along with a forwarded video. My mother is not shy about using caps lock or sending three lines' worth of emojis. Unlike my father, she's a technology savant. She has two phones and three SIM cards all serving different purposes and is a part of approximately 571 WhatsApp groups. She uses stickers, GIFs, bitmojis, and things that I didn't know were possible on WhatsApp. One of her favorites is a sticker of a woman threateningly holding a flip-flop. My sister regularly delivers speeches via text. A dozen or so messages announcing an update in her life, "I might go to taraweeh prayer tonight." A thought, a feeling, a story, or just a collection of statements. "Did you hear Swaziland changed its name?" she pondered once to no response.

It's also a source of support. When *Documented*, a publication I founded with a friend of mine that covers immigration in New York City, went live, I notified "My Family." They quickly latched on to my photograph on the About Us page, where I look like I'm auditioning to become part of a gospel rap group.

It's 11 a.m. in New York and I'm at our space in Chelsea, a fancy restaurant that is used as a coworking space during the day, while it's the evening in Beirut and my parents are likely sitting on the couch tapping away at their phones while the news plays in the background. My sister will likely be knocking off from work, heading to meet some friends for a coffee or a drink in Brussels.

> Mum: Mabrook. Great job. Allah y'wafiqak. What's with the beard though, I didn't recognize you?
>
> Me: Haha, thanks mama. I do need to shave my beard. I found a Sudanese barber in Brooklyn.
>
> Mum: No do not shave it, it is nice. I really like it. It suits you.
>
> Me: Thanks! I'll just clean it up so I don't look like a Salafi.
>
> Mum: Hahaha. Did u move or not yet?
>
> Me: Alhamdulillah. My new apartment is great but the cat is a little crazy.
>
> Mum: Do you have a cat? [facepalm emoji]
>
> Me: White people love cats.
>
> Mum: What do you mean?
>
> Me: It's my roommate's cat.
>
> Mum: Aha now I understand.
>
> Sister: WOW WOW WOW. I can't wait to see this. You look like a hipster jihadi by the way.
>
> Dad: Alf alf mabrook ya Mazin. Inshallah more and more success. Actually Mazin you look like a philosopher.

More than just laughs, "My Family" is an anchor that helps me wade the waters through difficult times. It's a form of something that has been elusive throughout my life: a sense of home. As a family of asylum seekers, the concept of home was broken from the very beginning. My parents' political activism meant that it was untenable for them to stay in Sudan when al-Bashir came into power. In a search for prosperity, we sacrificed stability. Moving from city to city, from country to country, building resilience but leaving pieces of ourselves behind. My parents sought to build a life for us while also pursuing their career goals. That's why we moved to the UK, to Canada, and why they keep moving into their sixties.

We're a close family. We genuinely enjoy each other's company. But sometimes I'm struck by how completely I can get lost in my life and what's in front of me. I could go weeks or months without speaking to my family on the phone. It is a great source of guilt and confusion. WhatsApp serves as a grounding device.

My parents were not able to attend my master's graduation. They weren't granted a visa due to an Obama-era rule blocking people with European passports who had visited Sudan from receiving an ESTA. I instead provided them live commentary of the event via "My Family."

At the reception following the ceremony, I awkwardly shuffled around as everyone else was stationed with their families. I was obsessively staring at my phone and hating myself for caring so much that my parents were not there.

> Me: Hey, how was the doctor yesterday?
> Dad: Hi Maz. The doctor got the result and said that there's something they want to be sure about; therefore he recommends that I do another image or biopsy.
> Me: Ok. Alright. Let's talk about it on the phone.

Many immigrant children carry a feeling of indebtedness to their parents. They sacrificed so much to ensure you had a better future and you promise yourself that you'll be there for them when they need you. When you can't, it hurts even more.

A few weeks later, my mum gives us another update.

> Mum: Hi Family, how is everybody? Good news. Dad got his blood test back and the result is amazing. He saw the doctor yesterday and he said he could start the radiotherapy at any time, it's up to him.
>
> Sister: Ok [thumbs-up emoji] Alhamdulillah.

One thing that transient families are often deprived of are memories. Pictures and family videos get lost in one move after another. Keepsakes slowly disappear as you start fresh over and over. But we always have the "My Family" WhatsApp group. It's an ongoing living archive of my mum's favorite stickers, a puppy throwing love hearts out of a box, four years' worth of my dad's bad jokes about "my president," Donald Trump, my sister's long speeches, in essence—our family history.

MAZIN SIDAHMED is an award-winning journalist and cofounder of *Documented*, a nonprofit news site that covers immigration in the New York area. Before founding *Documented*, he was a reporter at the *Guardian* (US edition) in New York on the national desk as well as with the award-winning Guardian Mobile Innovation Lab. He started his career covering the Syrian refugee crisis in Beirut, Lebanon, for the local English-language newspaper the *Daily Star*.

What It Takes to Make a Dream Come True

BY HASS AGILI

Sitting on the stoop of the town house where I live in Greenwich Village, I saw two guys walking along the street holding hands. They stopped just a few feet away from me and kissed each other. That was the first time I had seen such a thing happen in daylight, in the street. I felt happy, liberated . . . and a bit aroused. Well, imagine spending four and a half months in a refugee camp in a remote city in eastern Slovakia. That was a really dry spell, you guys.

I had arrived in New York City the day before, after a grueling thirty-six-hour trip that included thirteen hours of layovers. And now I was seeing rainbow flags everywhere, half-naked men, loud music, and I said to myself, *Man, you landed in the best spot.* I had no idea it was Pride weekend. I thought, *Is this what New York City is like? Gay and loud.* It was the end of June 2016. I had been a refugee for two years, moving from country to country. I was reportedly the only Libyan refugee to be admitted to the United States in 2016.

Growing up in Libya, I never felt I belonged there. Or rather, other Libyans never made me feel I belonged there. I was different. I had different interests. My fascination with languages began at a young age. I was watching CNN aged seven, trying to pick up any word that I understood. They broadcast a speech by Hillary Clinton, who was the First Lady back then. I heard her say the word *family*. She said it differently from the way we had been taught in school. Back at school, I waited for the day that word would come up. It happened a few weeks later. I was reading aloud, and I swear I could hear a countdown in my head—three, two, one, Hass, go—and I went for it: "family" with full American intonation. The teacher was confused. "Why are you saying it this way?" she asked. I told her that this was how they pronounced it on CNN. I got into trouble that first time, but from then on, she made me the first student to read any new lesson. So I decided from that day on I would just say words the way I heard them on TV. That is how I achieved fluency in the language, with an American accent.

I was an A student, usually first or second in the class at a military academy that was considered to be the best high school in the country. It was very strict and students were rigorously disciplined. I graduated among the top ten in the nation, which meant I could go to any university I wanted. I chose medical school at the University of Tripoli. It had been a dream of mine since I was five years old.

In 2010, I was in my fifth year of medical school, and a few exams away from graduating and getting my MD, when someone I had considered a friend borrowed my laptop and went through my emails, browser, and hidden files. He found some private communications I had had with other men, and he outed me at the university. Things were never the same.

I was bullied, discriminated against, and threatened. Being outed in Libya meant that I would be shamed, thrown out of school, and that my life and the lives of my family were in danger.

I realized I could not change the whole culture and its values and beliefs by myself. I determined, however, that I would not let that culture change who I am. For my safety, I took private lessons outside of school, and I moved to another city to take my final courses. But after the Arab uprising in 2011, the religious extremists and ISIS took control, and gay people were being executed. My fundamental safety was in jeopardy, which prevented me from taking my last exams.

In August 2014, there came a very dark, hot night. We were without electricity for about nine hours. I had just come home from a thirteen-hour workday as a manager at the Apple store, feeling drained and also devastated. That morning, I had seen a video of one of my close friends, another gay man. He was dragged down the street, put in the middle of the packed soccer stadium, and beheaded.

That night I decided it was time to leave. I packed a few things in a small bag. I did not say goodbye to my family. I wanted to spare them the pain of what I knew was likely a permanent farewell. With the only ticket I could get, I flew to Jordan and from there to Lebanon, where I would spend the next two years.

In Beirut, Lebanon, I went to the office of United Nations High Commissioner for Refugees (UNHCR) to apply for asylum. Along with thousands of refugees from Syria, Iraq, and a few other Middle Eastern countries, I went through dozens of interviews. I had to become my own lawyer because I could not afford one.

I prepared my case carefully. Despite the uncertainty, I

persisted, hoping I could navigate the complex bureaucracy. The irony was that I spent all my life hiding the fact that I was gay, and now I found myself having to prove I was gay. I wished I could just say to the officer, *Drop your pants and I will show you how gay I am*—but you can't do that.

Applying for asylum was one of the hardest things I have ever done. I was asked questions about the most intimate aspects of my life, over and over, to make sure I was telling the truth. It was the first time I had talked—to a stranger, in an Arabic country—about the fact I was gay. I was terrified, but I found enough courage to speak up and tell my story. I managed to secure my refugee status. Shortly after that, I learned that I would be one of the one percent of refugees worldwide who would get a chance to be resettled in a so-called third country. But I had to wait for such a country to accept my application.

Then one glorious morning, I received a call from the resettlement office of the American embassy telling me that my file had been picked up by the United States. I had a series of interviews at the US Embassy Resettlement Office. However, for security reasons, Homeland Security no longer conducted the final interview in Lebanon, as it was a political hot spot. Instead, they flew me to Slovakia, where I stayed for four months in a refugee camp and went through more interviews and medical checkups. Almost ten years earlier, I had met the American writer Andrew Solomon. My university professor had invited me to dinner, because a journalist for the *New York Times* was coming over, and he wanted my help with his English. Andrew Solomon had given me his business card that night, and for my final interview in Slovakia, he provided letters of support. He was instrumental in saving my life and getting me here. Adding to that, he has been housing me here in New York since my arrival and has made me part of his family. It was his stoop I was sitting on, the day after I got here.

Shortly after I arrived, my story broke, because I belong to nearly every minority group the new administration was targeting. President Trump had enforced a travel ban on citizens of Muslim countries including Iran, Iraq, Libya, Somalia, Sudan, Syria, and Yemen, and many Americans were outraged. My mother had called me asking, "Does that mean I won't be able to visit you ever?" After the travel ban was implemented, I was invited to appear on CNN and then on some other networks, to tell the story of how I came to be the only refugee from Libya to make it here that year. I decided to go ahead and do it, because, after all I went through, I thought this was the best way to announce that I was gay. I wanted to talk proudly about my experience as a gay man and as a refugee. I thought it was necessary to put a face to the United States' divisive story, to explain the truth about the grueling refugee resettlement process, and to bear witness to what it takes to arrive in this country. I wanted to share what it meant to be a new American, not just a refugee anymore. Weren't most of us in this country refugees or immigrants at one point or another?

Additionally, I wanted to reach gay people back home and in other oppressive countries. CNN has a wide reach, and my interviews reached both gay and straight people there. I anticipated the hate and backlash, which arrived promptly. I almost lost my family—they hadn't known the real reason I left was because I was gay; they thought I was seeking a better life away from the destruction that was happening in Libya. I lost the few friends I had left in Libya. But I also experienced a lot of love. I remember getting a message on social media from this guy who said; "I am a conservative Republican, and I welcome you. I also want to lick you all over your fuzzy body and face."

I was also contacted by many gay people in Libya, telling me that they consider me a hero. I don't know about heroism, but I know I inspired in them the knowledge that maybe one day they can be safe, happy, and free.

Now when I walk around New York City, I still can't believe I am here, that I made it to a safe shore. But I left many behind, which is something that breaks my heart.

I have been dating this guy lately who's sitting in the audience tonight. We walk around the city and he holds my hand sometimes. Sometimes he stops and kisses me. And every time, I can't help but feel the same: happy, liberated . . . and a bit aroused.

HASS AGILI was born in Tripoli, Libya, in 1983. He is the oldest of seven children. He went to medical school in Libya and was a few exams away from graduating before he had to leave the country for being gay. He arrived in the United States in 2016 and was the only Libyan refugee who was admitted that year. After almost three and a half years of trying to pick up where he left off in medical school, he was asked to restart his studies. Finally, in 2020, he started his journey as an undergraduate at Columbia University, New York, where he is majoring in neuroscience. He is no longer dating the guy mentioned in his story. After waiting five years to be eligible, he applied for US citizenship in March 2021.

Is This Thing On?

BY APARNA NANCHERLA

I've always felt at a lack of words. You can't tell from my writing. I have "can I speak to a manager" levels of entitlement when it comes to generating run-on sentences, but don't be fooled; it's not so much a carefully choreographed verbal flash mob of coherence, as throwing all the paint at the wall, hoping at least one relevant drip will stick. I hide behind flourishes and other unnecessary turns of phrase. It's certainly easier to embellish on paper than out loud for me, and it always has been. A hesitance with self-expression isn't necessarily that surprising when you're born the child of South Asian immigrants, or born an anxious, shy, introverted, highly sensitive creative type. What makes it unique, perhaps, is that I've chosen to primarily trade in words. I'm a comedian most of the time, and an actress sometimes, a writer other times and "prominent on Twitter" was once written about me in a blurb. All these crafts deal in communication above all else, typically in words.

When I was a child, my mother was constantly concerned about my general functionality as a human. I was very shy, and generously fearful—not at all choosy about what might stoke the flames of my dread. Reasonably: the stove, matches, fireworks, thunder, lightning, drugs (in my defense, this was at the height of the "just say no to drugs" campaign), swallowing pills, ghosts, violent criminals. Less predictably: riding a bike, most sports involving balls (but also ice skating and roller skating), big dogs, most cats, cool kids, sticking out, fitting in, talking to strangers or any authority figures, talking in general outside the confines of a very limited inner circle (three at most, at any given time, oftentimes stuffed animals).

My well-intentioned mother made a concerted effort in reforming me. Everything became a test, progressed through a different level of "being a capable person in the world." This gauntlet likely mirrored her own journey into official adulthood. My mom and dad are both first-generation immigrants from Hyderabad in southern India. They're doctors. He, an anesthesiologist, she, an endocrinologist, who both came to the United States in the seventies when there was a need for medical professionals here.

My father emigrated here first, tested the waters, and then returned to India to have an arranged marriage with my mother, who he later brought back with him. My mother was still finishing med school when she gave birth to my older sister, who was raised in India for the beginning of her life. Two years later, my mother had me in Washington, DC, when she was still working on her internship, and then she was completing her residency while she was raising the two of us, a true savant of multitasking. All this to say, my parents had a lot to learn, and fast, about how to make it in a brand-new country.

They lived in a variety of cities in a short amount of time, depending on where my father found work: Houston, Texas; Chicago, Illinois; Brooklyn, New York; and finally, the suburbs of Washington, DC. Imagine getting married to, essentially, a stranger when you're barely twenty-one and have only ever lived with your parents, and then leaving for a new continent to start a new life with that person. There probably aren't enough words to capture everything you're feeling and thinking, and not just because you're caught between languages—the one you need to fully embrace, and the one or ones that become secondary to survival. I think that's why my mother wanted to make sure I had enough words, because she didn't always have the luxury of them, when she first got here.

Nor did my dad for that matter. I remember interviewing him about his first experiences in the States for a family tree project in elementary school. Everything took adjusting to: the language, the food, the people, the culture, the very state of being. He once ordered a pizza and didn't realize how big a "medium" was, so he got up and moved to a different table when the waiter brought it over, assuming there had been some kind of a mistake. Still, he gradually took to American culture, even if it was on his own terms. Much to the horror of xenophobes, he loved country music because he found the song lyrics easy to follow and often evocative of the same "work hard, dream big" mentality of countless immigrant stories. His favorite song was "One Piece at a Time" by Johnny Cash, a resourceful ditty about an autoworker who fashions his own Cadillac by sneaking home one car part at a time from his factory job. The hustle was, and continues to be, so real.

When my mother joined my dad later on, there were

things he had figured out for the both of them, but there was still plenty to be learned. Add to that the pressure of raising two young kids, and it was no wonder my mother doubled down on her anxiety.

My sister was the more outgoing of the two of us. After all, she was the oldest, and the oldest usually takes on the role of trailblazing. She often ended up being the mouthpiece for both of us, forging friendships in our suburban cul-de-sac of a neighborhood, and accompanying me in school when I needed to talk to one of my teachers one-on-one. But my mother saw through this benevolent front of older sibling interventionism and decided I'd better shape up, or . . . shape up. There was no "ship out" option. Truth be told, she perhaps foresaw her own anxiety in me and wanted to make sure she wasn't sending out a baby bird without a pilot license. No way, not on her watch. I didn't even have the words for anxiety until a much later age.

My mother wasn't cruel or unusual with her methodology of disappearing my fear and helplessness. At first, she had me tackle existential and introspective activities like swallowing pills or turning on the stove in a home-school-safe-space-type-environment, but this quickly escalated into more advanced territory, like—perversely enough—talking to strangers. That's how I found myself the official household member tasked with ordering pizzas over the phone. (I don't know why pizza is an ongoing developmental theme in my family, but let's just go with it.) Our order was usually always the same: Pizza Hut, two mediums, hand tossed, one with green peppers and onions and one veggie-lovers—a classic Sunday night meal for our family. I distinctly recall pizza taking the edge off the dread of having to return to school on

Monday morning, but having to order it was its own tiny *American Horror Story* before the reward.

Another hurdle my mother decided would be beneficial to us all was putting my sister and me through public speaking classes with a group called Toastmasters. Needless to say, these classes were not marketed toward our age group. In fact, we were by far the youngest ones in the class, everyone else being full-grown adults, but my mother decided public speaking was a timeless skill, especially for a ten-year-old soul like me. This was also, I suppose, how I ended up in junior Jazzercise. My mother noticed I had no desire or affinity for physical exercise, and in combing the Community Center pages she stumbled upon junior Jazzercise, which was essentially an aerobics class for older women, scaled down for the elementary school set. It was unclear why this class was ever created, but in a pre-Zumba world, it was both marketable and horrific at the same time. Not only was the class right after school on a school night, but it was hard for me to get to on time, since my private school got out later than all the public schools. So not only did I not know any of the other girls in the class, but they found my case additionally unacceptable since I was consistently late, often trembling, and had to wear my mandatory school uniform to do aerobics in because I didn't have time to change. I was also the lucky kid in class who always got partnered up with the instructor's four-year-old son—who tagged along and knew all the routines by heart—since none of the girls would acknowledge I existed. Wherever you are now, I thank you, sir.

All these imaginative and dynamic tactics that my mother employed to ensure my eventual metamorphosis into a social butterfly backfired in one critical way. Each time I was dragged into the public square, the idea of sticking out became more and more abhorrent to me, and I strove to avoid it at all costs. It was so much easier to be invisible than draw attention—at the very least there were fewer eyeballs judging you. I proceeded despite the fact that undercommunicating could lead to situations that demanded far more explanations. I'm thinking of the time when I missed the bus home from school and my teacher tried to drive me home and my failure to both know how to get to my house but also how to communicate that fact led to us driving in circles for what felt like months in my kid brain. Still, it was always easier to primarily live in my head, not out in front of everyone else's.

My mother believed strongly in her efforts, and she was nothing if not a crafty and patient foe. She knew each of her tactics was a building block in making me the person she hoped I would one day become. I don't think either of us could have guessed this person was a comedian, but hey, neither of us knew there was a career option where you could smoothly channel your childhood emotional scars into using humor as a defense mechanism.

But if you put enough pressure on coal, eventually it becomes a diamond. And if you put enough pressure on a quivering human sponge, eventually she performs in basements at night for the approval of strangers. Because finally, after all those years of forced group grapevines and hostage-takeout-Italian-food situations, that sponge decided she had something to say. But it had to be on her terms. Because that's the only way to truly communicate: when it's not being forced or coerced out of you, and you decide it's finally time to share a few thoughts about what you make of all this. When you finally have enough words that you need and want to be heard—so much so, that you aren't afraid to tap the microphone and ask, "Is this thing on?"

APARNA NANCHERLA is a comedian, writer, and actor based in New York. She can be seen on Comedy Central's *Corporate*, Netflix's *The Standups*, among other places, and heard and read here and there. Aparna is currently working on a book, and yes, that's the loose definition of working. She's also available to house-sit for you, by which she means sit in her home.

2

Then and Now

An Alexandrian alien can't shake the nostalgia bug;
an intersex activist escapes Zimbabwe with dreams of
acceptance; a Bangladeshi rule breaker examines her battle
with modest dress; a Somalian in Australia considers key
moments over time and place; an eight-year-old's lifelong
passion is sparked by a robotic dog; a South African teen
with a purple suitcase leaves one apartheid for another

Stories by André Aciman, Tatenda Ngwaru,
Abeer Hoque, Khalid Warsame, Noël Duan,
and Magogodi oaMphela Makhene

The Nostalgia Bug

BY ANDRÉ ACIMAN

When you're a displaced person, there comes a moment when you realize you're not just displaced. Or that this stretch of new land is not your home and may never be, or that the idea of home, or of a homeland, has now become a completely hollow, unfamiliar concept to you. The new home is unfamiliar, but the old home itself becomes ever more unfamiliar—especially once memory and imagination have started muddying the waters and have allowed the old home to drift further and further away from you.

You are no longer an alien just to people who are no less alien to you, but you begin to feel alien to yourself. As if there is another you that was left in a cloakroom somewhere and for which you've lost the stub, and you're just impersonating him. As if identity itself is now in question, or lies in wait for you in some other, hidden dimension. As if you've lost your footing on planet Earth, but are no longer sure that you ever *had* a footing on planet Earth.

You are always going to remain a stranger among these new people. The language they speak, their sense of humor, which you can't begin to fathom, the strange currency they use, and the weird nicknames they give to each coin: dime, nickel, penny. The way they respect or fail to respect punctuality. The way they define space in a crowded subway car. The way they do or don't apologize when their elbow grazes yours in an elevator. The way they talk back to a film being shown in a packed movie theater. Down to simple conventions that are considered polite in one world, and unspeakably rude in another. Each one of these alienates you.

You will always be alien. Here and, eventually, back home as well, should you ever go back, only to find you are less of an alien in your acquired home than in the one that witnessed your birth. "Alien," for those who need reminding, comes from the word in Latin *aliēnus*, from *alius*, meaning "other." You are other than who you are. You are another, as the French singer Georges Moustaki—my fellow Alexandrian—says: "Je suis un autre," I am another. You're defined, really, as a minus. As a "not them," which ends up also meaning "not I."

At some point you are not only displaced physically, you are displaced psychologically, existentially. Being unlike others eventually implies questioning who *we* are, and when we ask this, we no longer know, much less trust, who we are. We are, as we realize over time, always in two places at the same time. We could be walking on a street, and suddenly, a scent—oh yes, I know this scent. It reminds me of our garden just before summer started, half a century ago. And how about this intense sunlight on a scorching sidewalk in Manhattan? It summons up a similar sidewalk thousands of miles away. By now, you know exactly what to do with this street corner, that flower shop, or this rotisserie because they remind you of others almost identical elsewhere. And this person's smile, and her way of speaking, the way she raised an eyebrow when I made a silly joke, surely she comes from where I come from—I can tell—she is one of us. If I ask where she's born, I know exactly what she'd say. And yet none of this is what I wanted to bring up here tonight.

Tonight I want to talk about a very private moment. It occurs before the sickness called "feeling alien" has finally rooted and defined itself. I'm talking about the period *before* you recognize the symptoms, before you even know when they are likely to strike, before you know in which ledger and under which archive to lodge your memories of the old country. Before you've ascribed memories to a Dewey Decimal System number. Before you've acquired the nostalgia bug.

There was a time in my life when the nostalgia bug hadn't declared itself, and wasn't catalogued, or even studiously pursued. There was a time when I was with a girl one late-spring day in New York, and suddenly, I was on the Mediterranean. There was a time when we bought food for breakfast in the Bronx, and on the way back, in the sun, I was not *just* in Alexandria, but also in a French film I'd seen that reminded me of Alexandria. But I wasn't hounded by all this. There was a time when I was happy to experience life without a past tense hovering over my shoulders. There was a time when I didn't know I was remembering— I thought I was living. Little did I know in those days that I was just reliving. How I wish I could just recapture those days. How I wish the writer in me hadn't intruded on them and allowed them to bait me at each turn.

One Sunday morning I called my father. He was living in New York and I was in Boston. It was an early-spring day and the sky was clear. He was going to play tennis he said, and he'd decided that even a sweater was not going to be necessary. It was almost sixty-five degrees in New York and in Boston. The day seemed so clear, so quiet on that morning that I couldn't help reminding him that this was a day for the beach, not tennis. He thought awhile. "Yes, you're right," he replied, as though it hadn't occurred to him at all. "It *is* a beach day," he said. I was just pulling a card out of my Dewey archive of memories. He, on the other hand, was living in the present.

ANDRÉ ACIMAN was born and raised in Alexandria, Egypt. He is the author of *Find Me*, *Eight White Nights*, *Call Me by Your Name*, *Out of Egypt*, *False Papers*, *Alibis*, *Enigma Variations*, and most recently *Homo Irrealis*. He is the editor of *The Proust Project* (all published by Farrar, Straus and Giroux). He teaches comparative literature at the Graduate Center of the City University of New York. He lives with his wife in Manhattan.

True Identity

BY TATENDA NGWARU

I almost didn't come here, because my father is not well back home in Zimbabwe. But then I called my mother, and she said, "Remember why you are there. You have to get up and go," so I ended up coming. Thanks, Mom.

My name is Tatenda. I was born intersex. For those who do not know what that is, it is a condition when a child is born with ambiguous organs, and the doctors cannot tell which sex the child is. Some intersex people have less obvious variations, and never know they are intersex. Estimates say that as high as 1.7 percent of children are born with some variation to their reproductive anatomy.

I came to America seeking asylum because in my country, my condition is regarded as shameful, and a laughing matter. Also—because being intersex is tied to the LGBTQ community—it is regarded as illegal. The Zimbabwe government carries out campaigns against LGBTQ people, and there are no protections against discrimination and violence. Intersex people are bullied and convinced to never reveal their true identity, which causes rejection, endless pain, and often, suicide.

When I was a child, my parents did not know the term for my condition was intersex. In Zimbabwe, we do not have doctors who are specialists in this field, so they did not have advice or information for my parents when I was born. Because it wasn't affecting me healthwise, my parents decided to raise me as a boy. They were confused, but as parents their instinct was to protect their child. They always showed me love and tried to protect me.

I got my first period when I was in school, wearing a boy's uniform. In Zimbabwe, boys have to wear boys' uniforms and girls have to wear girls' uniforms, which is annoying. When I got my period, it was evident to my parents that I was a woman—even though I knew already. I never doubted it. It's just that I didn't have any tangible information to prove it. So having my period was—in the words of my shero Miss Oprah Winfrey—an "aha moment."

I had to change schools that same week because every student was bullying me and drawing pictures of me on the boards and making fun of my body. At the time, my parents convinced me to keep living as a boy. They did this to protect me, because they knew the community wasn't going to be kind. The reason why I am standing here is because of my parents. I cannot imagine a world where I could have survived without their support.

But the bullying continued, even though I dressed like a boy. I was developing boobs, which I would bandage so that my chest wouldn't show. I read an article in *Cosmopolitan* about trans people, and that felt somehow familiar. Maybe I was trans? It was the only term that—sort of—explained what I was going through. During high school, I started dressing like a woman. At home I would wear unisex stuff. When I became a young adult, around sixteen, people started being aggressive. My parents didn't let me go out of the house after 6 p.m. They told me not to go to bars, because I could meet drunk people who could hurt me. I didn't like being told what to do, of course. But I always knew no matter how much we disagreed, when I was home, it was going to be a safe space. I felt I could always go home and feel their love and feel protection.

After going to college and obtaining my business degree, I moved to South Africa. I wanted to work, and go on my journey to find out who I am. I knew I could probably find a doctor who would be able to give me more information. I went to a doctor who worked with trans people and I asked him to help me. He was able to examine me and immediately tell me that I was intersex.

After a few years in South Africa, I came back to Zimbabwe. I founded an organization called True Identity, for intersex and transgender people. Before I knew that I was intersex, I had been living as a transgender person, and I wanted to support the trans and intersex community, which was largely in hiding. True Identity was the first organization in Zimbabwe promoting our rights. Word got around. We had secret Facebook groups, which is where I met people who had been living in hiding. I received funding from overseas. I tried to create a dialogue between the community and the transgender and intersex people, to create understanding and awareness and to try to normalize it.

I was physically and emotionally abused for this work. Sometimes the police would raid our offices to try and find the names of people that I was recruiting. People I didn't know would approach me and make ignorant comments saying I was an "abomination to the culture," asking me why I was "bringing Western culture to our country," and telling me "You are the reason we do not get rain. You are a taboo." I felt my life was in danger.

What really made me decide to leave Zimbabwe was when I realized my work was going to harm not only me, but my parents. One day, some people gathered outside our house, yelling. They knew about my organization and had found out where I lived. They wanted to burn down my father's house while we were inside.

My father gave me his last dollar and said, "I will buy you a ticket. Go somewhere where you will be accepted as a human, and a citizen who deserves human rights." At the time, Obama was still president. My father said: "If Obama hears of you, he is going to meet you, and you will change the world together." Oh, the dreams and hopes of a loving father for his queer child!

All my life I have worked with hope, faith, and instinct, so I thought: *This is my best bet.*

America is the land of dreams. That's what we hear in the music and in the culture. My favorite person is Ellen DeGeneres, she has her own program—and she is a lesbian! I watched Oprah Winfrey my whole life—a Black woman on-screen, killing it—and I thought, *Wow, this is a country that I want to go to.* What the television shows portray, and what I believed, is not exactly what I found here.

I had sixty dollars in my pocket when I came to this country. When I got to Los Angeles, I didn't know anybody. I got out of the airport and used the sixty dollars to go to the Los Angeles LGBT center. I said, "I am homeless. I have no dinner tonight, I have nowhere to sleep. Would you please help me?" I was told their policy does not allow them to help individuals. When it comes to housing and resources, they do not help. The only available resources are legal help and health. I slept outside the center for two nights. They wouldn't let me sleep in the building; maybe they thought I would rob the place.

Then I wrote on Facebook and said I needed help. A stranger said he would buy me a one-way ticket to New York. I started couch surfing when I got here. *What did I get myself into?* I often asked myself. I didn't have a job, I didn't have any money. As an asylum seeker, I was not allowed to work. It took me a year and a half to get work authorization and Social Security. And Donald Trump said immigrants are the ones that are doing illegal stuff on the street. How do you expect them to live when you don't let them work?

In America, instead of being welcomed with open arms, I felt ignorance. I discovered that many people did not know what intersex means, even within the LGBTQ community. The LGBTQ community was where I was supposed to find sympathy and be allowed to have a say. Instead, I would find out about events and pitch myself—"I hear you're doing this, would you mind if I add my voice?" Not so many doors opened.

My heart was further broken after finding out about the intersex infants here in America whose decisions are made for them by the health facilities and their parents. In many cases, infants with intersex conditions are operated upon, even though the surgeries are not medically necessary. Sometimes, the infants are surgically assigned the wrong sex. I have met so many intersex people who cry over their bodies being violated when they were children. Intersex people feel robbed of their rights, and body, after this happens. This further silences them and makes them feel powerless. This is happening, as we speak, here in America and across the globe. Even though my condition was met with ignorance and discrimination in

Zimbabwe, in some ways, I consider myself lucky in the fact that there were no doctors who specialized in my condition. Nothing was taken away from me until I could make that decision for myself, and until I knew who I was.

The more I found out about this country, the more I realized my work was just beginning. All I want to do is speak, educate, learn and grow, and raise awareness. I want to raise intersex awareness. I want to help protect the rights for intersex people. I want to help protect intersex children from medically unnecessary surgeries. The only way we can break the barriers is to familiarize people with what it means to be intersex. It is biological. It is not a choice.

I have met many intersex people in America. Many of them are not openly intersex. The ones who are, are mostly white. For intersex people of color, things are more difficult. We are not represented in the media, or anywhere else. If you don't see anyone who looks like you who is celebrated and who is out and free and happy, it is very scary. I believe that most intersex people of color fear the judgment that will come to them if they are open about being intersex. In this country that celebrates Oprah and Ellen, I hoped I would be celebrated, or at least seen. Instead, I feel ignored.

As a Black woman who is intersex, and an immigrant, and an asylum seeker, it sounds as if, right now, America's system was built to strike me down. But still, I decide to rise like an eagle. Ignorance, hate, and stigmatization do not bring me down because I know I represent so many voiceless human beings who live with so much pain. In fact, it gives me the strength to want to break those barriers. It is my only purpose for living.

Intersex awareness day is on the twenty-sixth of October. Tell your coworkers, your friends, your lovers, your parents, even your enemies. Light a candle with me on this day, and demand rights on our behalf that we never should have to fight for to begin with.

Not a day goes by that I do not miss home and my parents and the love that they gave me. I want to go back. But it is not possible at the moment. There is a documentary about me called *She's Not a Boy*. The people who made it traveled to Zimbabwe to film my parents. I saw the rough cut of the documentary and it broke my heart to see my parents, because I hadn't seen them since I left two years ago. I haven't gotten my asylum yet, so I cannot invite them to visit. Getting asylum takes years. I can now work, but I cannot travel outside the country. I cannot see my parents. All these things weigh on my brain every morning when I open my eyes.

Watching the documentary was upsetting, but I am happy people will get to see my foundation, which is my family's love, and hopefully see the importance of family in everybody's lives. My parents loved me unconditionally, and their love is the reason I am here. I choose to build beauty out of pain, so that anyone who is struggling will be inspired by my resilience. I want to continue speaking so that other immigrants who are in this country, or are planning to come here, will know they are not alone. I want to continue speaking so that any person who "has" something that society says they should be ashamed of will know that nothing can ruin your spirit. It is your world to conquer. It is your platform to demand a seat. It is your freedom to claim.

———

TATENDA NGWARU was born in Zimbabwe. She is an asylum seeker and intersex advocate. She is the founder of True Identity, the first intersex organization in Zimbabwe that promoted community awareness of intersex issues. Ngwaru has collaborated with Shondaland, has written for the *Huffington Post*, *Vogue*, and the *Root*. She is the subject of the documentary *She's Not a Boy*, a 2020 official selection at Wicked Queer: The Boston LGBT Film Festival.

On Modesty

BY ABEER HOQUE

A recent trip to Bangladesh made me think about the concept of modesty. Modesty generally refers to being unassuming or moderate in one's behavior or comportment. In my Bangladeshi Muslim immigrant family, modesty has always been about what we wore—modest dress. In Islam, both men and women are supposed to dress modestly, but as we all know, rules apply very differently to men and women, no matter what religion you are. My little brother could wear pretty much whatever he liked, but for my sister and me, modest dress meant no short skirts or shorts, and definitely no cleavage.

As a teenager in Rust Belt America, I subverted these rules as much as I could. I left my house each morning wearing long baggy sweaters and jeans. Before homeroom, I'd go into the bathroom, which was filled with girls shaking giant aerosol cans of hair spray and spraying their permed hair. This was the '80s, and so these weren't trial-size beauty supplies, but huge cans of Aqua Net that girls would lug around in their purses, kind of like '80s mace. I'd sneak into a bathroom stall, unpeel my "modest" layer of clothes, and waltz off to class in whatever midriff-baring top and miniskirt I had stolen from the mall. I'm sorry but I was an incorrigible shoplifter in high school (please don't tell my parents). After school, I'd head back to the bathroom, put my modest layer back on, and get on the bus, back in disguise.

In college, things got a little easier, at least when it came to my clothing. I just had to make sure there weren't any photos with scandalous outfits visible when my parents visited. These were the days before Facebook and social media made everything you did public, so that even your mom could see.

As I got older, I started to care less about modesty, and even less about religion. My philosophy of life, my religion, if you will, was about gratitude and celebration. My clothes were more outrageous than immodest, including that unfortunate year where I wore tie-dyed long johns in mixed company, like, all the time. Thank God there was no Instagram then. I would have never lived that down.

All this freewheeling living meant that when I moved to Bangladesh in my thirties, it was a real struggle to bring modesty back into my life. I was there on a Fulbright scholarship to take photographs and write, but the actual experience of living in Dhaka was a story all its own. One of the most common South Asian outfits is the shalwar kamis, which consists of a kamis (a dresslike tunic) worn over shalwars (baggy drawstring pants). The third part of this outfit is the orna, which is a long scarf that can be worn in a number of ways. Most traditionally, it's draped in a V or U shape across the chest and over the shoulders, nominally covering one's breasts. Lots of women wear it close around their necks like a choker with long tails. It's also often draped over just one shoulder. Note that most of these styles don't really cover the chest.

I managed the cultural paradigm shift from crop tops to kamises just fine. After all, I attended Bangladeshi dinner parties with my parents all the time in America. But I have always found the orna really annoying. It doesn't stay put, sometimes falls off a shoulder, hangs unevenly, or drags. It feels fussy. Then one day, I saw a woman, originally from the Chittagong Hill Tracts in the south of Bangladesh, who was wearing her orna totally differently. She had tied two adjacent corners and slung the knot across one shoulder like a messenger bag. I loved the look and immediately appropriated it. Not only did it stay put, even when hiking, but it was actually more modest because it covered all the naughty bits.

At first, I wondered why more women weren't wearing their ornas this way—it was convenient, modest, *and* interesting. Eventually, I realized that ornas were often more a gesture toward modesty rather than the thing itself. Plus tradition had cemented certain mainstream styles of wearing one's orna.

There are indigenous tribal people all over Bangladesh: the Chakma, Garo, Marma, Tripura, and many others. They have different mother tongues (though they often learn Bangla), and distinct customs, food, clothing, and religions, none of which are part of the hegemony of Bangla-speaking Muslim culture. Of course, the way they wore their ornas wasn't going to be the norm. It was fine, I told myself, if wearing my orna in this way garnered unwelcome attention. It could be my own private honoring of indigenous tradition. Anyway, I was already a weirdo in Bangladesh with my tie-dyed curly hair.

About two years into my Dhaka life, I met a woman who had dispensed with the orna altogether. I was shocked and awed. Her kamises were tailored to her buxom body, and there was no voluminous piece of fabric to hide any of it. Not only this, she was a spitfire, and if anyone looked askance or dared to say anything, from the old man in the park to the female shop attendant, she would curse them out in perfect, shocking Bangla slang.

It would take me another year to follow suit, because of my own ingrained concern about what people would say. Also, I did kind of want to belong. Over time, I came to understand that belonging takes place more in your mind than on your body. In the last seven years, I have gone orna-less in Bangladesh and America. In America, I dispense with the shalwars to boot, wearing kamises and dresses bare-legged, or with leggings in the winter. All of it feels normal, in the same way that modesty, like belonging, is a state of mind. If you think it's fine, it's fine. If you don't, there's no telling you otherwise.

These days, Bangladesh is heading toward a more conservative state of mind. Wahhabism, the puritanical Saudi strain of Islam, has had an outsize impact on the Muslim world. It happens directly through the Islamic institutions that Saudi Arabia funds in countries like Bangladesh, and indirectly through the migrant workers who toil in the Middle East and return to their home countries with Saudi notions of propriety and dress.

The national dress of Bangladesh for women is a sari. The shalwar kamis was the domain of little girls who would "graduate" to a sari when they grew up. But nowadays, women mostly wear shalwar kamises, and you usually only see saris at weddings and fancy events.

Every single woman on my father's side of the family is now wearing a hijab (in addition to the shalwar kamis and orna). Just ten years ago, none of them did. It appears to be by choice, but what is choice when faced with the zeitgeist? There are more burqa-clad women on the streets of Dhaka now than during my mother's time. It's dispiriting, considering my grandmother's generation fought to end purdah, the oppressive practice of hiding women from sight and society.

A few Decembers ago, I went to Bangladesh with my parents to attend three different family weddings. Because I've been going back and forth so often, I have my own networks and routines and haunts. This includes the veritable coup of being able to stay with friends instead of family. It means I get to sleep in, write all day, meet relatives in the evenings for dinner, and then come back for a gin and tonic before bed. Win-win-win-win.

The relatives getting married included two nieces and one nephew, all on my father's side of the family. All told, my parents and I attended nine different wedding events. The South Asians who read this will be unsurprised. I wore saris to each of these events, borrowing number after gorgeous number from my friend Neeta's incredible collection. One of the many nice things about saris is that they are one-size-fits-all. The blouse that is worn with the sari, however, is another matter. I owned one black sari blouse that had been custom-tailored to me years ago. Black, I figured, goes with everything. However, I had not really thought through the optics of wearing the same blouse to nine events in two weeks. When she realized, my mother asked me if I had any other blouses. I had to break the bad news. She and everyone else would have to see this blouse nine times.

But what I was initially more concerned about was whether this blouse was modest enough. It was sleeveless because sleeves make my armpits sweaty. The halter-top style left the entirety of my shoulders bare. And like most sari blouses, it stopped right under my breasts, revealing my stomach and back. On its own, it could easily be considered scandalous, and even with a sari, it showed a lot of skin.

All my cousin sisters and aunties would be in hijab. Would I be showing up at each wedding event not only immodestly dressed, but culturally clueless, or worst of all, rude? In an attempt to address this potential disaster, I took the anchal of my sari, the decorated part of the sari that goes over the shoulder and falls long in the back, and I wrapped it around my shoulders. We were having an unusually cold winter in Dhaka, and so it didn't look odd.

My niece Sadia's first wedding event was her Ga'ye Holud, a colorful, flower-power, song-and-dance extravaganza. When I got to the venue, the street was draped and canopied by fairy lights, hundreds of strings of lights that made everything look magical. I walked into the bright bustle of guests and bumped into my niece's mother, Momota Bhabi, a lovely, witty, modestly dressed woman. By the way, modest dress in Bangladesh does not mean sober or neutral colors. Momota Bhabi was wearing a hot pink sari with purple embroidery. Underneath the sari was a long-sleeve blouse that definitely did not show her tummy. Her hijab matched the purple embroidery and was fastened with a jeweled clip. Not an inch of skin showed other than her hands and her face.

I hugged her, and she hugged me back warmly, and then pushed me away gently to look at my outfit. I needn't have worried.

"How Bangali you look," she exclaimed. "And how beautiful."

I heaved a sigh of relief because my barely there blouse

had just been approved by the boss herself, the mother of the bride.

She continued, "Now, let go your anchal." Leaning forward, she unclasped my hand, and the anchal fell away from my shoulders and swung free.

———————

ABEER HOQUE is a Nigerian-born Bangladeshi American writer and photographer. She likes Hill Tract fashion, silver linings, and flowers in your hair. Her books include a travel photography and poetry monograph (*The Long Way Home*, 2013), a linked collection of stories, poems, and photographs (*The Lovers and the Leavers*, 2015), and a memoir (*Olive Witch*, 2017). She has won fellowships from the NEA, NYFA, and the Fulbright Foundation and holds BS and MA degrees from the University of Pennsylvania's Wharton School of Business, and an MFA in writing from the University of San Francisco. See more at olivewitch.com.

1993–2018

BY KHALID WARSAME

This piece was performed in Melbourne, Australia, May 2018

1993: A centipede crawls up a white wall, my body presses against the door, in fear. Water laps at my feet. This is the only memory I have of Nairobi, where we lived for a year before we came to Australia. Our first house there, a dilapidated two-bedroom unit in Flemington, also had white walls. When I ask my mother, she tries to remember if our bathroom in that small Nairobi apartment ever flooded, but she can't recall if it did. That whole time was a blur to me, she says.

2016: My phone rings too early in the morning. My mother on the other end. She has just woken up from a nightmare. She has been crying. "I just wanted to know that you're safe." She almost said "alive."

2000: I almost drown.

1995: My father holds my hand too tight as we cross the road to get to the children's hospital. He is explaining how I am due for a catch-up immunization, which means we have to go to the hospital instead of having a special day at school, where a giraffe named Healthy Harold (in reality a man in a costume) teaches kids all about vaccines and where the organs in our bodies are located, and how they could each fail thousands of ways. "Immunization," says my dad, slowly. I try to repeat it after him, but I stumble over the syllables. The hospital doors are wide and cardboard cutouts of cartoon characters dot the foyer. While we are waiting in line, someone drops a box—a loud bang rings across the atrium—a woman screams.

1997: Miss Ryan announces that we're going to do a project called "Family Histories." My classmates bring back photos of their parents, their grandparents, with proud stories. I get up and tell the class that we lost everything in Somalia during the war, so I don't have any photo albums to share.

1997: The first time I see the ocean. I find a puffer fish washed up on the rocks, so much smaller than I imagined it to be. The sea is wide, so wide, and ships glide across the horizon. The mouth of Port Phillip Bay is barely visible in the distance. March flies bite at my ankles, the only exposed part of me. My father fails to light a cigarette, his back to the sea to break the wind. He eventually gives up, and watches over us, distant and still. My mother walks up to the water and stares at it deeply, practicing its motions, before slowly dipping one foot into the sea, the outline of her body visible as her dirac is pulled against her by the wind. I'm older now than she was that day.

1998: My dad turns the channel to the news. Politician Pauline Hanson's maiden speech to parliament. She warns that Australia is in danger of being "swamped" by Asian immigrants, who "have their own culture and religion, form ghettos and do not assimilate." My mum scoffs. "They'll be after us next," she says.

1999: My brother and I find a dead baby pigeon on the ground and decide to bury it. My mother watches us as we fumble through some prayers and says, "You're supposed to dig the grave deeper, otherwise it will be exposed again."

1995: A man grabs my brother and pushes him up against a fence, turns to me and says, "You black dogs." I drop my lunchbox. My brother has already forgotten about the incident by the time we get to school.

2015: I lock myself out of my house and scale the side wall to let myself back in. A neighbor yells out at me. I turn to him and am suddenly struck by the fact that he doesn't recognize me. I tell him that I live here, that I've locked myself out. He has his phone out, like a weapon.

2012: My father calls me while I am in America. Almost by accident, we start talking about the war. "Your mother experienced it so much worse than I did," he says. Later I think about how that fact cast its shadow over so much of our lives.

2015: I'm on a date and I'm trying to figure out something to say. We're talking about how we construct identities, which is a pretty heavy topic for a date. I try to change the subject by telling a funny story about something that happened to me and a friend of mine. She doesn't laugh, but has a thoughtful look on her face. She asks me if I consider myself Australian. I think about it for a moment. I tell her that I've been told that I'm not Australian too many times in my life. It leaves a mark.

2017: I move back to Melbourne after five years living in Brisbane and visit an old friend who lives in Truganina, in the outer west. After lunch we go to pick up his car from the mechanic. A young Lebanese guy greets us. "What nationality are you, cuz?" I tell him I'm Somali. He cracks a smile. "You're a Somalian brother. Waryaa!"

2017: I'm at the beach with my friends. They all jump in the water together. I lag behind building up my confidence. The sea is so wide, so unimaginably wide.

1999: My uncle tells us that there's a jinn that has been possessing members of our family for generations. My siblings and I lose sleep for days, until our father sits us down and tells us that there is no jinn. The next night, the wind howls outside, and passing cars throw sinister shadows against the walls. My brother is convinced that we've angered the jinn.

2005: Abu Hamza, who leads Friday prayer at my Islamic high school, tells a story about how Allah saved the mosques in Aceh from the tsunami, how every other building was leveled. He tells us to open our hearts to our brothers and sisters in Aceh. That night I have a dream of being swallowed up by water, my family gone, the sea thick with bodies.

2006: I'm at the video store with Farah. I pick up a movie and show it to him. "How about this one?" Farah scrutinizes the cover. "Does it have any Black people in it?" he asks me. "I don't know," I reply. He looks at me like I should know better, and I feel like I've failed a test.

2004: Our Islamic studies tutor announces that there will be no classes next Saturday, on account of it falling on the anniversary of September 11. My friends and I cheer, happy that we get to have an entire Saturday free.

2015: I'm at a dinner party with a group of people I don't know very well yet. The guy sitting next to me tells me that he's reading *Things Fall Apart*. His partner, across the table, smiles proudly and tells me that she's making him read it. I tell him that *Anthills of the Savannah* is my favorite novel by

Chinua Achebe. "Oh, is that how you pronounce his name?" he says.

2016: At another dinner party, someone else tells me they're reading *Things Fall Apart*. I note the coincidence.

1996: I have a fight with an Indigenous boy in school, Tristan, and I break his glasses. His mother approaches my father the next day and asks that he replace her son's glasses. My father agrees, apologizes for my actions, and gives her cash. The school principal finds out and calls my father. She tells him that he shouldn't have paid her a cent. She calls the woman and her son "those people." My father brings up this incident often, whenever the conversation turns to white Australians.

2016: I get up onstage and do a reading. It's an ambivalent piece about our scars, and memories, and how they resist narrativization, and how we narrativize them anyway. Afterward, a woman approaches me and tells me how inspired she was by my words. I ask her what she means by "inspired." Inspired to do what, exactly? She gives me a baffled look, smiles, and walks away. A knot of guilt settles in me.

2015: I arrive in Puli Township in the rain. A man is waiting for me at the bus stop, a cigarette in his mouth, bent back, kind, warm eyes. I had found his website the week before, where he offered free lodging to visitors in return for some conversation in the mornings and evenings. He takes me to his home and shows me where I am to sleep. We communicate through Google Translate. Later that night, after I get back from a long day of hiking through the hills that ring the small town, we share a glass of whiskey and he begins to tell me about his time in the army. I don't speak a word of Mandarin, but I piece together his gestures and expressions, along with what little I know of Taiwan's history, into a vague outline of violence. He shows me a gray photo of his unit and points to each face and does a "throat-cut" gesture. Then he gets to the last picture, of a young man with kind eyes. He points to himself and then chuckles and does a throat-cut gesture again, as if to say that he, too, will soon be dead.

2018: I enroll in swimming classes, despite my fear of water.

———————

KHALID WARSAME is a writer and arts worker. His essays, fiction, and criticism have appeared in numerous publications. He has appeared as a facilitator and guest artist at writers festivals and his work has recently appeared in the anthologies *New Australian Fiction* (Kill Your Darlings), *Growing Up African in Australia* (Black Inc.), and *After Australia* (Affirm Press). Previously he worked as a codirector of the National Young Writers' Festival and creative producer at the Footscray Community Arts Centre. Occasionally, he makes radio with 3RRR and takes photos. He lives and works in the unceded lands of the Wurundjeri people of the Kulin Nation.

Good Dogs, Good Humans

BY NOËL DUAN

My first dog was from Japan. It was not an Akita. It was not a Shiba. It was an Aibo, which means "pal" or "partner" in Japanese. It also stands for artificial intelligence robot. This was 1999, I was eight years old, I was growing up in Silicon Valley, and Sony had just come out with a litter of robot dogs.

Aibo's likeness had entered my imagination long before the factory in Aichi Prefecture gave birth to them. In the fourth episode of *The Jetsons*, which first aired in 1962, Elroy, the son, really wants to get a dog—a real dog. George, the dad, is not convinced, so he comes up with a compromise. He buys a robot dog called 'Lectronimo whose benefits include "no feeding, no bathing, no fleas." He's nuclear-powered and he's made of metal sheets, with an antenna for a tail and no fur to hide his bolts and screws. George brings the robot home, and he finds out that the family got a real puppy, a stray named Astro, while he was gone. By the end of the episode they keep the real dog, and they donate the robot dog—to the local police station, which, nowadays, I've realized is a prescient observation of the future of artificial intelligence and law enforcement. But watching that as a kid, I noticed something else. The Jetsons live in the future (2062, to be exact), drive flying cars, and have robot housekeepers. They're very comfortable with using technology to replace the messier aspects of their lives. And yet, even they chose to keep a real dog. A dog that slobbers, has accidents, and sheds all over the carpet.

A few years after I watched that episode of *The Jetsons*, my dad, like George Jetson, brought home Aibo, my first robot dog. I had zero experience with dogs or pets in general back then, but I was obsessed with getting a dog. You know how every immigrant kid fixates irrationally on that one thing that they think will make their family American, whatever that means? Maybe it's having hamburgers for dinner? For me, it was getting a family dog—that's what I thought all true American families had. But my parents were disgusted by the idea of having animals as companions—you see, they grew up in Cultural Revolution–era China, where food was so scarce that my mom, for her birthday meal as a child, had a fried egg. It was the only egg they could afford all year. If you had an animal in your home back then, you ate it. My dad, like George Jetson, thought Aibo was a great compromise.

I fell deeply in love with Aibo. When you petted the touch sensors on his forehead—this was before iPhones so, touch sensors were very high-tech—his eyes lit up with love and he wagged his antenna tail. When you called his name, he stiffly walked toward you before bowing at your feet. I would whisper stories to him and his ears would perk up. My mom told me that the good thing about robot dogs like Aibo was that they would never die and leave me. But that turned out to be my first big disappointment in technology, which, looking back, was a good thing to have learned growing up in Silicon Valley. Because eventually, like a real old dog, Aibo's joints began creaking and he began moving slower and clumsily, with more effort. He didn't always hear me when I called. But when I petted his touch sensor forehead, his eyes still lit up. Aibo was my Velveteen Rabbit. He was real because my love for him was real. My love wasn't enough to keep him forever, though.

As with many childhood dogs, one day, Aibo just wasn't around anymore, and I didn't know why. But over a decade later, I found out where Aibo had gone—or, at least, for the sake of childhood me, where I hoped Aibo had gone. There's a 450-year-old Buddhist temple in Japan where Aibos are sent from all over the world to die. They arrive with letters detailing who their family members are and where they grew up. One of the temple's priests told *The Guardian*, "All things have a bit of a soul."

I got busy in high school and I moved to New York for college, and I forgot about dogs because I spent most of my time thinking about myself. Two years after graduating, I got laid off from my first job. For the first month of unemployment, I had trouble getting out of bed. So I thought, *You know what? I should get a dog—because it would take me on walks.*

I knew I would adopt a rescue puppy. I didn't care what breed—all I knew was that I wanted a puppy to begin a new life with me. She was shaking in my arms when I first held her, and she was the only puppy at the adoption event who didn't bark. She just sat there quietly, trembling, waiting. She had just flown up from the animal shelter in Miami the day before, and she was scared. And I was scared too. But I just thought, *Wouldn't it be nice if we learned to be brave together?* I named her Artemis after the Greek goddess of wild animals and young women.

The first night, Artemis had explosive diarrhea all over her new bed in the middle of the night. I carried both her and the bed to the bathtub to rinse, my hands covered in poop, and I was mad. Not at her, but at myself. I was twenty-five, I was unemployed, I had just broken up with someone, and I was covered in dog shit. I thought, *How can I ever become an adult? Who do I think I am, adopting this dog and taking responsibility for her when clearly I cannot take care of myself?* And I also thought, *George Jetson was right, having a robot dog is much easier.* But Artemis, still covered in diarrhea because it took more than a rinse to get that off, looked up at me with her big brown eyes, and I realized exactly why the Jetsons kept the real dog and not the robot dog. I knew I would do anything for her.

I moved to New York when I was eighteen for college, and I've been here a decade. I thought New York became familiar once I was able to confidently give subway directions to lost tourists. But when I got a dog, it was like a whole new New York opened up to me. I became friends with my neighbors— which is no small feat in this city. Every morning, Artemis and I go to Central Park for off-leash hours, and I catch up with the same dog owners in my neighborhood, day after day, year after year. Dogs are natural social lubricants because they have no hesitation about sniffing each other's butt. And if dogs greet each other by sniffing each other's butts, what's so scary about simply saying hello to someone?

Artemis always finds something new to explore on every walk we take, even when we're walking the same route around the same block, and I admire that about her. She reminds me that I don't know the world as well as I think I do—and that there is still plenty left for me to explore too. There's always something left to sniff and buried treasure to uncover.

I wanted to bring this community of mine online. So, in 2019, I launched a community for good dogs and the good humans they love, called Argos & Artemis. I tell stories about dogs and humans on my website. For example, my classics professor, Marcus Folch, always intimidated me. I earned my first-ever C on a paper in his class back in college and, because I was nineteen and easily mortified, I thought I'd graduate and, thankfully, never speak to him again. And yet, because of a quick email I sent him about Argos & Artemis, I got to spend an afternoon with my former professor and his German shepherd, Emmelia, and we had a two-hour conversation about how Plato probably had dogs because he mentions them so much in *The Republic* and how Professor Folch's childhood dog Honey died in his arms when he called her across the street and she got hit by a truck, and how he's never been able to recover from that loss. I started realizing that storytelling about dogs isn't just about dogs—it's about humanity. If you want to get to know someone, ask them about their dog.

I wasn't sure what my parents would say about Artemis. In fact, when I was adopting my dog, my mother actually called and warned me it was another big mistake I was making. But, the last time I was home, I saw her pull up a stool to sit with my dog in the hallway. She was talking to Artemis, and Artemis was staring up at her, ears perked up, much like how Aibo perked his stiff metal ears when I spoke to him.

———————

NOËL DUAN, a first-generation American born in China and raised in Silicon Valley, is a writer, dog mom, and founder of Argos & Artemis, the global community and lifestyle platform for good dogs and good humans with good taste. She was on the founding teams of Miss Vogue Australia (which was named Apple's Best App in 2013) and Yahoo Beauty (under editor in chief Bobbi Brown), and has been published in *ELLE*, the *Guardian*, the *Atlantic*, *Teen Vogue*, *Ars Technica*, *Stanford Social Innovation Review*, and more. She holds a bachelor's degree in anthropology and art history from Columbia University and a master's degree in women's studies from the University of Oxford. She always carries treats in her pockets—because you never know who you might meet.

Don't They Have Irons in America?

BY MAGOGODI oAMPHELA MAKHENE

It was one of those plastic suitcases sold as a bona fide knock-off at Oriental Plaza. A purple bag with a hard shell and zero compartments. My mother bought it using money that had more pressing jobs, like getting groceries and paying school fees. The suitcase carried the smell of ghee and fried peas in samosa triangles. Plus that clean crisp feeling that is Johannesburg in the clutch of autumn. My life arranged itself neatly inside. When it came down to it, all I hauled to America was a few changes of clothes, fresh towels, and a year's supply of toiletries. No joke—I had enough toothpaste, roll-on deodorant, and Nivea body lotion on me to boost a whole bodega. At some point, my mother wanted to buy me an iron. My grandmother—my mother's mother—a woman who only left her house to bury an important relative or to see about a new young doctor all her friends raved about at Baragwanath, she laughed. Don't they have irons in America? she asked.

Her son, my mother's youngest brother, my cool uncle

Benny who must've been growing his first stubble just as I was born; the heartbreak hustler with forest-thick jerry curls à la the Jackson Five and a tongue as slick as a snake's, *he* asked *me*, Aren't you scared? That question still stays with me. Because to me at seventeen, Benny's whole life seemed to outfox fear.

Take that one time we got stuck at a garage late at night. We were moving from Soweto to a white suburb, under cover of dark. I was ten years old. My father very freshly dead. Suicide. His family blamed my mother. She fretted, felt they had too much fertile energy for foolishness. This was a woman who'd taken to sleeping with an Okapi slipjoint knife under her pillow. Just in case. All around us, tension was tightening like a sticky blood clot locking around a heart.

Mandela was just now-now a free man. Still negotiating our future. Still heaving a whole country off the cliff edge of civil war using nothing but clever words threaded through his strong teeth. A schoolmate called Mandela a thug—an otherwise bright boy, this kid. I got into a verbal spat with him, reminding him all the things his family had stolen. He looked at me, confused. Like he wanted to cry.

—Bad people go to jail, he said.

—And now the baddest person in the world—a terrorist! gets waltzed out of jail and you lot want to make him president?!!

I remember it was sunny outside, that the windows were steel cottage frames, huge colonial gateways forever flooded with light. And it was quiet. Even the purple jacarandas seemed witness to my shocked discovery—a person could be as bright as this boy and still come out stupid. Not long after this exchange, the boy's parents packed up with the white flight; they sold the family house with the dishwasher and dog inside and gave away the maid and garden boy before shipping off. They left for the final frontier, Australia.

Others threatened to settle the score. These white nationalists mounted their horses and tried to raise a rudderless ruckus. We'd see them on the six o'clock news waving guns at empty rallies, looking like a band of Hitler's lost constables. It didn't help that our new neighbors looked like them. Wore the same drab knee-high socks, the same thick beards, khaki pants, and short-sleeve khaki shirts. My mother made light.

—Sies, she'd exclaim.

—Maburu a! I mean, in 1993? Who's still dressing like a prison warden on a field trip to the zoo?

—Look at those skinny shorts crawling up his flat ass, she'd carry on.

—Bona, bona—just look at that! A whole grown man. Otswere ke tswape?

—No, for real! she'd say, answering her own question. That's a wedgie!

—Imagine that! A full-grown man with a wedgie and a gun. He better know how to dig himself out without shooting off his ass. Not that there's much of it anyway . . . man looks like he's modeling hunting diapers for verkrampte types.

My sisters and I would bowl over—near dead—little hyena cubs attacked by hacking laughs.

And then we'd double-check the front door. We'd triple-check it was locked. And also the burglar-proof with its iron grille. We'd seal ourselves in for the night.

My mother didn't share her fears with us. I didn't know about the gleaming Okapi blade under pillow-stuffed feathers until many years later. Or the telephone calls at the old house. She didn't tell us rough voices spat vulgar threats into her *Hello?* The callers wanted her dead husband alive. They wanted her out of the house. They wanted my mother dead.

Leaving that Soweto house felt like a grand escape. My mother told no one. We packed after sunset. And called in Benny for reinforcement.

On the road, the car gave trouble and the garage attendant wanted money. Big money. My mother forked over whatever she had. My mother's little money. It could've been something simple stalling the old sedan, like running out of petrol, which had become so normal after my father died, that we rolled around Johannesburg with an empty canister in the boot. Just in case. And it could just as likely have been something dramatic; the car was no young buck and we were riding with an entire household loaded onto its back. I mean *shiiit*—I'd balk at that myself! Whatever it was, Benny convinces Garage Attendant Dude to sort out the mess, promising more money if he can just get the car to start. Money we don't have.

When the dude is done and it's time to pony up, Benny makes a motion for us to load back inside. To roll up the windows. And lock the doors. We do. Then he sloughs off the attendant like a banana shedding its skin. He moves like a cat away from the conversation and into the car. He starts the engine as if to check it again and revs the old Mazda. Still talking to the dude, still negotiating payment we don't have. Slow-slow, Garage Attendant Dude catches onto Benny's scheme. We are already leaving. He paces the now chortling car and chases, incredulous, running alongside the now moving and rolled-up windows, waving big threats and shouting furiously with both his hands, banging open palms and fists on the doors, as if big and fancy cursing ever throttled any engine. Demanding we pay.

All I remember next is Benny's body colluding with the moving car. And Benny's waist, and one leg and one shoulder riding halfway in the Mazda, while the other leg and half-butt dangled outside. I can still hear the screech of the car, careening out of the garage. I can still see Benny's dark and hairy hand on the wheel, eyes trained not ahead but over his shoulder. Somehow, he managed to fire up the old Mazda and drive halfway off *before* closing his door, his body only-just wholly seated, his beautiful brow and Jackson Five s-curl fully sweated. We peeled away, into the night and Mandela's promised land.

. . .

When I arrived, it was into 1999's golden bubble. And America was definitely the promised land. White men picked up my trash. I'd look out my California window and watch them work, jaw to floor. White men. Collecting my used tampons and pencil shavings and whatever else couldn't be swept under the rug. As a Black kid fresh out the can from apartheid South Africa, this picture looked like Mars. Or some lost future. And yet, I couldn't square its perfect plastic smell with nigglings of old familiar hang-ups glaring through the cracks.

In a public high school with over one thousand students, I could count on one hand the few brown bodies in my AP track. In our cocoon of suburban glut, my student exchange program host parents spoke about nearby Oakland like the devil himself pitched camp out there to stoke up fires. It's dangerous, they said. There's criminals. Gangs. *Their* drive-throughs are drive-bys. I knew this language. It had the same timbre and tone as words used to describe Soweto. By people who'd never been *over there*. Classmates and parents and teachers and the evening news. They'd say these things to my face, about a place and people I called home.

The next year, in Minnesota, I soon saw a pattern as a college freshman. Caribbean, Asian, and African international students like me were recruited to fatten the melanin count. Our campus was a short ninety-minute ride from the Twin Cities; where were all the Black students born and raised in Near North, Minneapolis? Why was the affirmative action quota not catching all those kids whose grandparents built Rondo, St. Paul?

I was uncomfortable in this promised land. Slowly and wearily, I remembered Benny's question. It rose up in my mind like stale air surfacing from algae forest farts. *Aren't you scared?*

In the land of a thousand lakes, people spoke about "Minnesota Nice." In hallways and between lectures, strangers made sure to grin at me if our eyes suddenly met, showing me all their many teeth. On weekends, the same kids hurled words like *Nigger* and *Go home* in slurred speech. He's just drunk, floormates said. He doesn't mean that.

One Saturday night, I was out with a friend. A crude-oil-black and beautiful man. A soccer fiend who turned his file-cabinet-style closet into a Ralph Lauren Polo shop—every plaid and short-sleeve shirt neatly tucked into perfect corners. The kind of through-and-through African-reared youth who laughed at our calculus teacher's corny jokes even as the rest of us sat comatose and timid or checked-out and fidgety. We were walking somewhere, me and this Polo shop soccer fiend. Passing a building with big windows overlooking the path. Someone was partying. You could hear the thump from below. And see their drunk and pasty face poking into the soft dark.

—Hey! the drunk called out.

—Dipshit!

—Yeah I'm talking to you, dipshit.

My friend looked up. It was early autumn. The days long, fat with gold foliage. Nights crisp but still inviting, no real hint of the white wilderness that lay ahead.

—I will fuck you up! my friend shot out, disappearing in his anger and planting into the earth. Heat rose up, I could feel it. Or maybe it was always there, like an electric charge that rides clean air. I called to him, to my friend. I wanted to leave. But he wouldn't hear of it. Not again. Not another time looking away. Swallowing another sting, pretending its sharp bite meant something else, something feral, yes, but toothless. He wanted the drunk. Writhing. Wanted his words and mouth in his fists, wanted to sober him up by gagging.

. . .

I came to America thinking that I was leaving apartheid behind. That neo-Nazis wearing diaper-fit khaki pants and white supremacist salutes were sealed into my rearview. I carried a hard-shell purple bag with nothing but my future packed inside—or so I thought. I have no idea what happened to that bag. It saw me through so much of these vast lands First Nations call Turtle Island—from California to Minnesota and Philadelphia, and well into a few years after college. It must've gone the way of used TVs I'd see Americans throw out. Or those perfectly good cars people donate in a land rotten on so much stuff.

That bag had many stories. And dead dreams surreptitiously sewn into the lining, a cheap nylon, also purple. Some were mine but many more were passed on the way a favorite aunt might leave a fat wad of rands from her laundry job at the bottom of the family's first college-bound niece's luggage. Until the money—useless in a foreign land—thins into hairy mold. Maybe that's what Benny meant when he asked, *Aren't you scared?*

Of so many unanswered prayers? Of tattered dreams handed down like curious heirlooms?

Growing up, I watched Benny and his entire generation lose parts of themselves they didn't even know they had. Like having everything inside you to make the Olympic swim team, but being denied the pull of water on your limbs. Having that flightlike moment when the body remembers it is water, snatched from you. Because you were born into a choke hold designed to squeeze all your insides and imagination out, a system made to stamp out any promise or potential you showed beyond the lowest station "where you were meant to be—as a hewer of wood and drawer of water," as apartheid's chief architect, Hendrik Verwoerd, argued to parliament. Verwoerd, who got his peers to scrap rigorous science and math in Black schools in favor of Bantu education, a dumbed-down curriculum that emphasized subjects like Bible study and gardening. A violent miseducation whose widespread and pernicious claws still suffocate South Africa's economy today.

Benny and his siblings, including my mother, all his friends and peers, they all grew up on a first-name basis with this choke hold. Benny was always curious about our schooling. He'd pick us up from school and ask, What are you learning? How will you apply this to a future world? I'm not sure Benny ever finished matric. His high schooling career was one long stay-away followed by states of emergency—a violent white supremacist state clutching to power while a restless Black populous fought back tooth and nail with sticks and stones and sneers and spears. Most of his cohort didn't finish school. My mother can still count on one hand which of her friends in all of Diepkloof—a neighborhood numbering tens of thousands—passed their matric exit exams.

I never asked Benny what he wanted to be as a kid. But I do remember an unfinished conversation about what could have been. He was listening to my sisters and me going on about school. About the white teachers and white kids. About the many small and daily nicks: *What kind of name is that?* To the grander, stupider, more nakedly racist ideas. *Mandela!?! A crook?* We laughed. Swimming class came up. We weren't big fans. Too much havoc on our hot-fried hair. Benny just listened. Quiet.

Only now, it occurs to me how young he must've been. How close to us in age. Our gated private school world, just then opening up to Blacks, could easily have been his. And how foreign too. I'd be surprised if Benny encountered any white child or adult he could openly challenge before Mandela's release. And by then, Benny was a man.

He wanted to know what swimming class was like. Could we swim? Did we practice after school at the new house? And then he started a sentence about things apartheid stole. He never finished that sentence.

My uncle is well over fifty now. He's never had a formal job. Never learned to swim. I haven't seen him in years. I know there is a soft residual bitterness lingering in his bones. How could there not be? He was once a bright and promising man. My vain and curious uncle. Apartheid choked most of this out of him. Left him carrying that massive brain like a dusty volcano so long idle its death is mistaken for dormant.

When I left for America, it seemed I'd hit the jackpot.

Yes, South Africa was changing, Mandela and then Mbeki, president. But white supremacy remained (and still is) ubiquitous, written everywhere in sharp invisible ink. I'd escaped through a back door. I could be anything in America, the Promised Land.

Anything except caste-free. Benny knew this. He saw ahead. To the America that would greet me, with its fancy apartheid fooling no one.

—Aren't you scared? he asked.

—Of what? I said, weighing his question with a question.

—Flying. Who do you know who's been flying?

—You, I said. Remember that night? At the garage? You were flying that night. Don't you remember?

MAGOGODI oAMPHELA MAKHENE was born and raised in Soweto and is currently completing a collection of interwoven short stories exploring the inner lives and loves of ordinary South Africans making a life in a time and place most often inhospitable to their journeys. She's earned fancy awards like the Rona Jaffe Foundation Writers' Award and the Caine Prize for African Writing. Outside writing, Magogodi is cofounder of Love As a Kind of Cure. She lives in Cape Town and New York.

3

Deep in New York City

A New Yorker remembers the 1970s glitter scene and the kings of underground rock; a cursed woman seeks aid from a Dominican Santera in the Bronx; nannies in Central Park air their grievances; a heart attack survivor lets her heart lead her home; war enemies unite in a Manhattan maternity ward

Stories by Xavier Trevino, Xochitl Gonzalez, Christine Yvette Lewis, Dr. Hisla Bates, and Sofija Stefanovic

The Table of the Kings

BY XAVIER TREVINO

I only saw David Bowie perform once, and that was in June 2002 when he was on *The Today Show*. Working as a night porter at the time, I'd get off work at 7 a.m. The morning of the gig, instead of heading to my apartment in Hell's Kitchen from my job on the Upper West Side, I headed to Rockefeller Plaza, to see David Bowie for free.

The crowd was already big when I arrived, but there was a good view of the stage. *The Today Show* cast was below my line of sight, and I could only hear their banter in front of the stage, where Katie Couric and the gang talked to people and read the weather. Eventually David Bowie was announced, and he came onto the stage amid a lot of clapping and cheering.

He looked good, dressed very simply in a light leather jacket. I don't remember any of the band; I mean, why would you when there's David Bowie to look at? They played three or four songs, only one of which I recognized, "Fame." I'd stopped keeping up with Bowie in 1979. That was the year of a great transition for me. I ended up homeless because of my increasing drug addiction, and two years in the army did not stop my downward spiral. By 1983 my drug use had blossomed into a monster heroin habit I did not kick until the year 2000. There's no room for niceties like going to see live music or spending money on music when you're an addict.

I first heard Bowie in 1972 when I was eighteen, when they started playing "Ziggy Stardust" on WNEW FM. But it wasn't until after I'd seen the New York Dolls for the first time on New Year's Eve 1972 that I got *into* glitter rock. It was the music I was waiting for all my life. The clothes they wore, the attitude of studied insouciance (displayed especially by Johnny Thunders, the New York Dolls' lead guitarist) was very appealing. They had what I wanted and were more accessible than Bowie or Lou Reed, who were big stars on a big stage.

My love of glitter rock was well-established the first time I heard Bowie's "The Jean Genie" in my friend Eddie's room in the dorm at Pratt in early 1973. I'd gone to see if he was interested in buying coke, and he said he wanted $10 worth.

"But I only have grams, it's $100 for a gram."

"So give me a tenth of it and I'll give you ten bucks," he said.

I had to lay it out on a piece of broken mirror he'd conveniently placed on a table and divide it into ten parts. He took his ten dollars' worth and then produced a syringe, a spoon, and a glass of water. But first, he put the 45 rpm single of "The Jean Genie" on the turntable and cranked it up. He mixed the cocaine with water in the spoon and drew it up through a cotton ball into the syringe. He shot it up.

"Give me another ten," he said.

It went on like that until he'd spent the $100, and "The Jean Genie" played at full blast incessantly, over and over again for probably an hour. I was fascinated by his shooting up and said I wanted to try it. He told me he didn't have another syringe and wasn't going to share his.

"Get one and I'll show you how to do it."

A few months later Eddie and I went to see the Stooges at the notoriously exclusive Manhattan night spot Max's Kansas City.

I'd seen the Stooges once before at the Pavilion in Flushing Meadows Park in Queens when I was fifteen. Back then, I'd never heard of the Stooges, or of Iggy Pop, but I had cousins who had, and they were very keen for me to see this new band. At home I'd grown up listening to classical music, Mexican folk music, and Broadway show tunes. My father was partial to classical music, and he would conduct symphonies wielding an invisible baton in front of the hi-fi when drunk. The show tunes were catchy, and my mother's beloved Mexican ballads took work to listen to.

My cousin Francine was seventeen, two years older than me. Her mother was Mexican, like me, and her father was Puerto Rican; but she and her sister, Lana, had been born here in the States, they were "real Americans," unlike me. Lana and Francine took it upon themselves to be my mentors, teaching me the ins and outs of being a real American teenager. And American teenagers listened to rock and roll. (A year earlier, my sixteen-year-old Puerto Rican upstairs neighbor, Edgar, had tried to mentor me to be a Latino teenager. He had taken me to a salsa dance at the old Hotel St. George in downtown Brooklyn, and I didn't like it. He tried to teach me how to dance the cha-cha, but I was too uncoordinated or too removed from the Latin beat to do it properly. To me, it was Puerto Rican culture and I couldn't relate.) But when the Stooges started playing that hot night in Queens, the beat of the drums and snarl of the guitars reached deep inside of my viscera, and I was home. My cousins and I started writhing and shaking in time with the music, and I felt I'd found myself. It had nothing to do with being Mexican, Puerto Rican, or American, just what was inside of me. It felt free and inclusive. I could writhe and shake like everyone else to my own beat and not any formal cha-cha steps.

Aged nineteen, going to Max's Kansas City with Eddie, I was excited to see the Stooges again. I'd bought the *Raw Power* album when it came out and played it incessantly, and I was going to be able to see the band in a small intimate venue instead of from a hundred feet away with thousands of other people like at the Pavilion in Queens four years before.

I was a veteran of a dozen New York Dolls shows and had morphed into a glitter rocker from my hippie days. Teased hair and high-heeled shoes were the order of the day. What struck me as funny about the whole glitter scene was the collateral fallout of how a lot of the Mexican immigrant service workers in the city quickly adopted the platform-shoes-for-men style. Just the shoes, not the makeup and glitter. They were, on the whole, shorter than the average American and wanted to look taller. I was tall for a Mexican, and for me the heels were just part of making the scene.

The Stooges stormed onto the stage and ripped into "Search and Destroy," and Iggy shook and jumped and launched himself into the audience using my thigh as a stepping-stone. It was a seventy-minute frenzy of sound, sweat, and skin.

All too quickly the show was over, and I found myself standing on Park Avenue South with Eddie. I heard people talking about an after-party.

"Let's go to the after-party, Eddie."

"I don't think we're invited."

Two Quaaludes and two Bloody Marys told me otherwise. "I'm sneaking in."

It took me a couple of tries but I finally made it past the guy at the door and I was mingling with the likes of Lou Reed, David Bowie, and all the New York Dolls.

It was like being in a dream, all my idols here in one place. Now if I could only interact with them. At one point, Lou, David, Iggy, and Todd Rundgren were sitting at a table together. The kings of underground rock. It was exciting and intimidating at the same time.

Out of all the people at the table the one I most wanted to talk to was Lou Reed, who was a hero of mine. The moment he was alone I walked over and sat across from him, and just as I opened my mouth to speak, I felt a hand on my shoulder. I looked up into the big round face of a very large man who informed me in a West Indian accent that "Mr. Reed doesn't want to be disturbed." I wasn't so taken with David Bowie at the time, so I settled on following Iggy and Johnny Thunders from the New York Dolls around. I followed them into the bathroom, where I could hear them sniffing something in one of the stalls. Johnny gave me a dirty look when they came out.

Just as I was about to go home, having run out of cash, I went to pee. Someone came in and stood at the stall next to me. It was Iggy.

He had ditched his stage costume for the party and was clad only in a tight silver lamé miniskirt, and nothing else. He was barefoot. He lifted the skirt to pee and looked over at me.

I was frozen; here was one of my rock idols taking a leak next to me and he was looking at me. I smiled, keeping my eyes on his face.

He stared at me with those blank Iggy-eyes, and finally said, "I'm so fucked-up, man."

"I think you are great," I blurted.

He grunted and looked down to check on his progress. He finished, shook off the last drops, and strode away without another word.

A few years later I was in the East Village punk dive CBGB's one night watching the Dead Boys. The friend I was with nudged me and yelled into my ear, "You're standing next to David Bowie."

I turned to look at the man standing with his shoulder pressed against mine. He looked like David Bowie, but he was just wearing a T-shirt and a jean jacket, so he couldn't be the flamboyant David Bowie.

I yelled in his ear, "Hey man, what's your name?"

"My name's Frank," he replied. But he couldn't hide that accent.

Watching Bowie that warm summer morning in 2002 made me look back at the steps that brought me there. Johnny Thunders and Jerry Nolan of the New York Dolls had become heroin addicts like me and had paid for it with their lives. Lou Reed was sick with hepatitis from drinking and shooting speed. Iggy had gotten clean and written a song about it, and I believed Bowie's own struggles with addiction were under control. In 2000 I finally gave up the life of drugs and "went straight" like Iggy says in the song "Look Away."

A few years ago, Bowie died. He's gone, along with Lou Reed, and so many others. I just read a Facebook post comment under a picture of Iggy with Johnny Thunders where the commenter wrote, "Iggy turned Johnny on to heroin. If I ever met him I'd kick him in the balls." Obviously, the guy who wrote the comment has no idea of what it's like to be a slave to chemical dependency, and the kinship you feel with fellow addicts. I don't know how to explain it, but there was something in the music these guys made that resonated in my soul, that feeling of desperation and thirst only addicts know. And when you hear that, you feel like you are not alone. I wonder how Iggy feels about being one of the last kings at the table.

XAVIER TREVINO was born in Mexico and immigrated to the US as a small child. Growing up in Brooklyn he attended the prestigious Brooklyn Tech High School and went on to study film at Pratt Institute on a scholarship. This was when addiction took over, till he got clean at the age of forty-six and rekindled his love of writing. He has taken writing workshops at the JCC in Manhattan and has a WordPress blog in addition to working on a memoir of growing up out of place.

The Limpia

BY XOCHITL GONZALEZ

The day that I sat in the waiting room full of other cursed women, I did not know exactly who had cursed me, but was doubtless I'd been blighted. My heart had effectively stopped functioning, you see. Everything it touched turned to terrible shit, and also, inexplicably, I had a pain in my hip bone anytime I tried to dance to reggaetón, which in those days was quite often.

I suppose no one ever truly knows who curses them. It's all speculation. Gentleman's witchcraft—the kind with robes and wands and boarding schools, where the person looks you in the eye, points their wand, and curses you to your face—that didn't happen much where I'm from. Magic had been driven underground, generation after generation, so that now when you heard about it, it was almost always whispered in the negative. Usually related to, as in my case, a harmful curse. Always anonymous. Of course, I had my suspicions as to who had hexed me, namely my soon-to-be-ex sister-in-law who had rumored ties to Haitian voodoo, which, though loose, weren't loose enough for my tastes. I concluded that Haitian witchcraft was best countered with a strain derived from another part of that same island and found a Santera from the Dominican Republic who saw patients in the Bronx.

I don't want to say that there are more brokenhearted women in the Bronx or anything. I mean, who am I to say? But I will say that in el Bronx, the good Santeras have such volume of business that they run their shit like an HMO and you need a referral to even get an appointment. At Sylvia's, Mondays and Wednesdays were diagnostic readings. On Tuesdays and Thursdays, standard treatments. Fridays were for miracles. I did not need a Friday ritual and I was very grateful.

My first trip, on a Monday, had been relatively expedient. I left my house at 8 a.m. for the hour-plus train ride uptown. I arrived around 9:15; *¡Despierta América!* was on and before it was over, I'd been diagnosed. My heart was broken because of my mother. This is totally true. And somehow, someone had cursed my hip to stop me from dancing with joy. Yes! My sister-in-law! And finally, I was haunted by the spirit of a lost love who still yearned for me. Sylvia wasn't sure if it was a curse or a haunting—she explained that she could cure me of the first two but not the last. She would try, but there were no guarantees. Her daughter who doubled as a receptionist scheduled me in to come back on a Thursday at noon, with a dozen roses, a red candle, a change of clothes, and two coconuts. *Para una limpia.*

The Thursday visit was less time efficient. I sat with my candle, clothes, coconuts, deli roses, and exactly $57.72 in an envelope on the plastic-covered floral sofa in the impossibly large living room with a dozen other women, all in various states of distress. I knew this because almost all of them were talking on the phone, loudly, about what had led them there that day: jealous coworkers, romantic rivals, hostile siblings, shortness of funds, and general streaks of bad fortune.

A handful of children, toddlers mostly, played in a corner, watched over by the bruja's other daughter. The apartment was kept at an islandlike 75 degrees, and so, despite it being late October, we patients had stripped to various states of undress. Today the TV played old episodes of *El Clon*. At some point, when I had been waiting for a couple of hours, plates of food—habichuelas guisadas and ensalada con aguacate—were distributed. *This*, I thought, *does not happen at the doctor's office*.

"It's crowded today," a middle-aged woman next to me volunteered. "Sylvia leaves soon for Florida, everyone wants their limpia before she goes."

A snowbird, I thought. Witching was good business.

Periodically, women would be called in, and between forty-five minutes and an hour later they would emerge wet-headed and radiant, buoyant bundles of energy that, taken collectively, began to lighten the anxious mood of the large living room. These women—freshly cleaned—moved about as if in the early stages of love, when it all felt good and harmless. I wanted desperately to feel that way again. I tapped my thigh in anticipation with one hand while shoving food into my mouth with the other.

No two limpias are exactly alike, but some elements are consistent. At some point you will get completely naked. Sometimes, the Santera washes you. Other times, you bathe yourself. Always, they pray over you. Always, there are offerings. Always, at the end, you walk out with a trash bag filled with your bad energy, which you will need to carefully dispose of. By now, I consider myself somewhat of a limpia connoisseur, and I say with confidence: Sylvia's were the gold standard. For it was only at Sylvia's where there seemed to be a process, where layer by layer you felt the curse washing off you, spinning down the drain.

First, Sylvia strips you naked, and then cuts up the clothes that you were wearing and puts them in a bag. She has you stand in her shower stall and she hands you a bucket filled with steaming hot Florida water, bay leaves, and eucalyptus. You pour it on yourself. Sylvia directs you out of the shower, so that she can gather the leaves that have collected in the drain and then place them, too, in the bag. Then, she impatiently directs you back into the shower where she slathers you in a mixture that, later, when sitting alone covered in it, you realize is just Mazola oil and sugar, but as she applies it, feels like spiritual sandpaper against your skin. She leaves nothing uncovered, methodically coating your hair, your eyelids, your earlobes, your breasts, your buttocks, your inner thighs, your legs, and the webbing between each and every toe. She tells you to hold on to her for balance while you raise one leg and then the other, so that she can scrub the sole of each foot. You don't know her at all, aside from the ten minutes you spent with her when she read your cards, but you feel safe with her. You feel she wants the best for you. Once you are fully coated, your eyes closed from the weight of the scrub, Sylvia places you in a folding chair just in front of the shower.

Now it is time for prayers and meditation. Her daughter, the receptionist, not the babysitter, comes in and joins her. They pray over me in Spanish. They light my candle. On this particular day they pray to Chango, the god of music and laughter, to get me dancing again. They pray to Yemalla to help heal my relationship with my mother. They pray to

Oshun to fix my heart and make things not turn to shit when I touch them.

They ask me if I want to listen to my meditation in English or in Spanish, and though I know I should say English, I'm insulted by the question and I reply in my poor Spanish, "Español, por supuesto." They laugh at me, say whatever I prefer, then press play on the English version. *God wants you to be happy*, it says. *God wants for you the best things that you want for yourself.*

Then, they leave me alone, covered in sugar and oil, with my thoughts. Eventually I hear the click of the stop button on the boom box and the incantation ends. Sylvia escorts me back into the shower stall, runs the water, and hands me a bar of soap and a bottle of Johnson & Johnson baby shampoo. "Rinse," she says.

It takes considerable work to get the mixture out of my hair, rinsed from my pubis. The shower stall tiles are pink, some missing. The water runs more hot than cold. It is the best shower of my life. At the end, Sylvia stands there, again with the bucket. "You rinse," she commands. "Use all of it. Put it everywhere."

I raise the steaming bucket up to my head. I realize that it's rosewater, the most pungent rosewater I've ever encountered. I pour it over my hair, onto my face, into my ears, down my back, against the soles of my feet and I feel truly content as heartbreak spirals down the drain.

As I emerge on the street in my change of clothes with my bag of spiritual trash and wet head, I pass another woman. "You must have had a limpia," she says. "You're glowing!"

When I make it back to Brooklyn, though it is early evening, I head to bed and fall into a deep lasting sleep, comforted by the scent of my skin, which inexplicably will go on to smell like roses for the next week, despite numerous showers.

XOCHITL GONZALEZ was raised in Brooklyn, New York, and is the author of the novel *Olga Dies Dreaming* (Flatiron Books). She has an MFA from the Iowa Writers' Workshop.

A Little Tattle-Tale Around the Nannying Gig

BY CHRISTINE YVETTE LEWIS

I came to New York summer of '89. From Trinidad and Tobago, a twin island that locals refer to as "Trinbago." A place
where masqueraders float across an enormous stage in wire-
bending costumes adorned with colorful plumes two days before Ash Wednesday. To rhythms of calypso and soca on soil
rich with petroleum. Where tourists come to find leisure by
pristine beaches to the sounds of steel drums playing sonatas
and Frank Sinatra's "My Way." Even hummingbirds, scarlet
ibis, and cocoricos twerk on fever-pitch air as they take flight.
The master calypsonian Mighty Sparrow's saucy refrain about
"Jean and Dinah" working for the Yankee dollar echoed from
every bar and tavern on Charlotte Street. The old bards drank
old oak and Johnnie Walker Red washed down with coconut water, all the while swatting fierce mosquitoes. A pan of
cooked-up rice with slivers of chicken thighs and feet sat on
a counter beside the bar for the famished among them. Not
forgetting some fiery island pepper sauce to flavor the meal as

they spit stories of "dem Yankees" who set up base in West Trinidad in 1941 and how this puny twin island wrestled the British for independence in 1962. Not forgetting son-of-the-soil Stokely Carmichael coining the phrase "Black Power" as he fought for civil rights in the United States in the '60s. As they say, "the things that will make you cry is what Trinis laugh about." Carefree, fun-loving people who really care. Mind you, if we had our way, every day in Trinbago would be carnival.

Two of my sisters were already making a life for themselves in the Bronx and they would every so often urge me to come to the States. My daughter had just turned four and I was finessing and updating my preschool knowledge to help her along. On top of that, I was teaching literacy classes in the evenings. While trying to develop my knack and love of ballroom dancing. I knew I had it in me to be all I could be: dancer, musician, actor, writer, organizer. America would be ready for me. The expansive stage of Broadway could handle me, or so I thought! My sisters knew I had it in me, too.

The morning was molasses dark when we boarded the British West Indian Airway to New York. The aircraft would be touching down in San Juan, and all passengers had to disembark to get on a connecting flight. My little princess's feet running right alongside mine as we navigated the airport. It was there where my grip ("a grip" is an old-fashioned way of saying suitcase) got broken. Five Puerto Rican guys smelling like cargo grease were laughing as if they were in the front row of a Comedy Central event. I gave them a razor-sharp stare, and with no time to spare, like a desperado, I took off the belt holding up my slacks and used it to secure my luggage. Whew! I blew a sigh of relief. A broken suitcase zipper had nothing on us. I reckoned that we were ready to face what was ahead. I was armed with my "Jesus and I" songs, Psalm 27, some well-worn prayers, and some unyielding faith passed down from my mother. We were ready!

The ride from JFK was nauseating. Water oozed from my pores like I had just been hosed down at a pre–West Indian Day Parade Wet-Fete. As the car navigated the tertiary streets of Chinatown, I could smell the residue of rotting food from those industrial garbage bins.

Among the decay, I was in awe of the ornate high-rises with decorated window dressings, and men who rushed to open doors of fancy cars—in uniform, resembling Buckingham Palace Foot Guards, without fuzzy bearskin hats. As the car came to a halt at the stoplight, men and women with paper cups rushed the window. "Can you spare a dollar, change, a piece of food, anything please?!" Then it dawned on me that these streets weren't paved with gold, much less milk and honey flowing from their gut.

We settled in nicely in my elder sister's apartment. The summer was finally waning and autumn was making her entrance. The cool air was made for comfortable nights and some thought-provoking conversation with self. I decided we were going to stay in New York instead of returning to Trinidad. But there was rent to be paid and food to put on the table. I had to help my sister. I needed clothing for myself and my daughter. The seasons were changing, which required me to have money, not traveler's checks. I needed bread. Period!

I got my daughter settled into a kindergarten program, then I set out on my journey to get a piece of the "American dream." One of my sisters said the *Irish Echo* was the "go-to" paper to find jobs. The ads were for babysitters, live-in helpers, elder care caregivers—a far cry from what I used to do. One day, I came upon an ad that wanted someone to look after a three-month-old baby on the Upper West side of Manhattan. When I got to the house, the woman said, "You are the seventy-fifth person I have interviewed." Just to think that seventy-five people are interviewed to take care of one baby is beyond me. I guess this happens only in America.

I said, "If I am the seventy-fifth person, then let me be the first person you hire."

She was a little depressed. But I was like a high-tension wire with a pep in my step. Confident for days. I believe my personality was much too much for her. But then, that's what she wanted for the baby. Someone who could take charge. As fate would have it, I was hired. I had to remind the mother that in order for me to take care of her "prized possession" in an efficient and effective manner we must seek to know each other. We don't have to be friends or drinking buddies but we must work together for the well-being of the child. She agreed. We had our misgivings, but we were able to work them out. I stayed on the job for six years.

New York took some getting used to. I got me some fancy sweaters and insulated coats with boots lined with faux fur. "Bring it on, old man winter," I'd say. I would dress the baby warmly and snuggle her in her stroller and I would navigate the Upper West Side. Taking long walks along the avenues, stopping to browse at designers' outfits in freshly decorated store windows.

Then I discovered Central Park, the "crème de la crème" of all the parks I had seen. And women who looked like me— brown—pushing alabaster babies in stylish Maclarens. I could hear their sugarcane accents, sweet, as they talked to their babies in the strollers. I followed on the footsteps of these women to the playground. Forty-Second and First Avenue had nothing on Ninety-Fifth and Central Park West. This park was truly the crossroad of the United Nations. There were women from Nepal, the Philippines, Trinidad and Tobago, Barbados, the Congo, Mexico, Peru, El Salvador, Bangladesh, England, Ireland, Russia, and Poland. I couldn't introduce myself fast enough.

"Lady"—you could almost twerk to every word that exited her mouth—"money and privilege can treat you like that. Dem people have no respect, no respect, whatsoever! None, none, none, none, none, none!"

A broken leaf bristled past her nose.

"Let me just say this, he doesn't have any money, it's his wife who is loaded. Anyway, this man, son of a bitch that he is, blew his Cuban cigarette smoke right in my face because I told him not to smoke the cigarette in front of the child. Can you imagine?! Should I have said anything, considering that I suffer with acute sinusitis? Baby Beth, the cutest little cherub—her cheeks cherry as plum tomatoes, as you can see. Look at her, she is only four months old. Girl, we aren't their parents, but we must be their voice and seeing-eyes. To top it off, those cigars smell like sour feet on a humid day."

"Excuse me, ladies! I couldn't help listen in on your conversation and I just had to add my six cents," she said. The woman who had joined the conversation looked a little like Frida Kahlo, except taller. "Can I tell you this is my fourth job in less than eighteen months? I don't know what these people want. They hire you to take care of their children and then they want you to drop their Balencia—bear with me, I can't pronounce the name of the designer—coat to the dry cleaners. Their shoes to the shoemaker. Launder their 350-count sheet and iron it! Sometimes you become the plumber, the dog walker. Mind you, the dog walker makes something like $15 for half an hour and I barely make $12 an hour for all the work I just outlined. On a given day I can be the pre-K teacher and a five-star chef all for small change. I can barely afford the rent, much less put food on the table. They cannot even begin to live on what they pay us. Slavery has been abolished how many years now, and I feel like nothing much has changed. Island folks have a saying, 'Why buy the cow when you could get the milk for free?' I feel like that's what some of these employers do. Most of us give up all the things we worked hard to achieve in our countries and we come to America in search of the American dream. Only to realize it is a farce. It is full of holes and deception. And by the way, what is the American dream? Whatever it is, I have learned it is not for the faint of heart."

Her charge, five years old, proud of his sandcastle, calls to her from the sandbox, "Rosie, look what I have made!" as he shovels sand into his pretty baby-blue pail.

"Anyway, this is my fourth job! You would almost think babysitting is like a walk in Central Park. Well, sometimes, it can be like eating bread the devil knead with his feet—hard! The parents make this job of caring for and loving their children so freaking complicated. While we're on that, let me just tell you why I got fired from those four jobs. The first job: my lady and I went strolling along the dank avenue one afternoon, it was to Barnes and Noble on Fourteenth. There is always storytelling for the kids in the children's department. You ladies know when you reach the curb you have to actually lift the front of the baby stroller to navigate it on to the sidewalk. Well, it seemed like that rubbed madam the wrong way. She said that she didn't like how the stroller rocked and ricocheted onto the sidewalk. It could have tilted over and her baby could have fallen out! Hon, that was the last day on my job.

"The second job? Well, one week in of getting comfortable with little Ben, madam demanded that I shouldn't eat what her son was not allowed to eat. Which meant that if her son wasn't allowed to eat M&Ms, I wasn't supposed to have them. Guess what? I love me some M&Ms. Take that!!! So I bought a pack from the nearby deli and got to taking care of the baby, forgetting the bag of M&Ms in little man's carriage. Over the weekend that woman called and said, 'You are a really nice woman, but we won't be needing you anymore.' And let me share this with you. You know how the parents emphasize reading to their kids? Just beware of some of those books. I say that because I was thumbing through Ben's bookshelf and I saw a book that had belonged to his mother—her name was etched on the front page. It was *The Oxford Nursery Rhyme Book*, first edition. Printed a couple of years before I was born. When I opened the book I really didn't know what to feel. It was riddled with racist nursery rhymes. Why would a parent have a book like that among her child's books? Just know that when you sing to the kids, 'Ten little monkeys jumping on the bed,' it really wasn't ten little monkeys jumping on the bed, and I will leave that right there!

"We are all coming from different places with different customs, practices, and beliefs. Some of us are the sole household providers and we put up with shit for all the wrong reasons. Some of us, our men are gone and so we put up with the disrespect and the derogatory name-calling at their homes just to provide for our children. Some of us are filling barrels with stuff to send back to our families. And ofttimes the pay isn't great. But some of us suck it up. Not me! I know my worth, so I ain't putting up with nobody and their bullshit. I am not taking crap from the man who breathes in my face at nights, much less my employer who don't pay me enough to watch their children!

"The third job? Baby Robert was five months old. He was as cute and round as the eyelet buttons on my baptismal dress. His biological mother was also of Jamaican descent like I am, which might explain why I loved him a little bit harder. You can just imagine how I doted on that little boy. His biological mother, discovering that she was pregnant at sixteen years old, made a huge decision to give him up for adoption. She wanted to pursue a scholarship in track and field. See, my lady's dollar could afford him, while she refused to pay a handsome wage. I worked from Wednesday to Sunday. From 8:30 a.m. to 7:30 p.m. While I didn't mind the work schedule, it bothered me that taking care of Robert morphed into washing this woman's clothes. Taking her miniature poodle for a walk so he doesn't stain her Afghan area rug. Washing her floors. Making her bed and dusting her furniture. She gave me a flat salary and nothing consistent with the minimum wage. December came and my heart was set on something extra, to purchase gifts for family and friends. She handed me a Christmas greeting card from her and Robert with some money in it. It was my regular pay for the week I worked, not a penny extra. I was used to getting bonuses from the other jobs I worked. I mentioned that, and she said, 'I don't know anything about that.' The following Wednesday the phone rang, I looked at the number in the window and I refused to answer it. From time to time, I think about Robert. I also think of how much it must have cost my employer to get him, and how she refused to pay me a decent living wage to take care of him."

"Hmm," said the young woman with the south of England accent. "One of the parents I work for shared my information with another mother. The woman emailed me with the job requisite. Let me read it to you—'For the baby's protection and mine I want you to get these vaccination shots: Whooping cough, Hepatitis B Vaccine, Hepatitis A Vaccine, Measles, Mumps and Rubella Vaccine, Documentation with Blood Titers of Measles and Mumps, PPD (Screens for Tuberculosis), Tetanus.' As if that wasn't enough, she wrote an encyclopedia of my responsibilities! Let me tell you, I refused what the doctor ordered. If madam and her husband ain't getting the shots, then why should I?"

New York was my new home, and it was at my new job, during these tattle-tales with the other babysitters that I realized we have to empower each other around what is acceptable and not acceptable in an industry that is rife with exploit and disrespect.

"What are these people thinking when they ask questions like, 'How do you clean a baby's behind? What would you do if the kid said an airplane came into the room and mowed down all the toys? How would you describe the fruit you gave to the child?' Huh?! Well, if they aren't afraid to ask you some of the most rambunctious questions, ask your own questions with integrity! 'Madam, if you hire me to care for your baby, just know that if you add on anything else—such as picking up packages from the post office, cleaning your baseboards, floors, furniture, silvers and lamps, changing light bulbs, running errands, doing your laundry, grocery shopping, planning and preparing meals as if I am a five-star chef—just note they are jobs all by themselves and do not fit the criteria of a babysitter. However, if you need your babysitter to fulfill those roles, did you know you will have to pay more? And much more! Guys, it was nice talking to you, I have to go and feed the baby. *Oh, how the wheels on the bus go round and round!* See you tomorrow!"

CHRISTINE YVETTE LEWIS is a leader/organizer/activist/secretary, cultural outreach coordinator with Domestic Workers United (DWU), who are nannies, elder care caregivers, and housekeepers in New York City. New York State was the first state to win the Domestic Workers Bill of Rights, which set a precedent for other states to go after their very own Bill of Rights. DWU is also the cofounder of National Domestic Workers Alliance (NDWA). As a worker-leader and multi-disciplinary performance artist Christine encourages culture and art as strongholds in the work for social justice and domestic workers' rights. She has spoken out on initiatives like the Domestic Workers Bill of Rights with Brian Lehrer of NPR and on *The Colbert Report.* Christine continues to organize domestic workers on the grassroots level, encouraging her peers to bring their voices to the continuous fight for justice.

My Heart's Journey Home

BY DR. HISLA BATES

My name is Dr. Hisla Bates, and I'm a board-certified pediatric and adult psychiatrist. I'm a mother, an artist, and photographer. I'm a writer, house flipper, SCAD survivor, and I'm an immigrant. I'm going to tell you a story about my heart's journey to find its way home.

In 2015, I had a spontaneous coronary artery dissection, or SCAD, a rare form of heart attack. At the time, I didn't know whether I'd live or die. I promised myself that if I survived, I would make changes in my life; and I would be forever grateful for the life that I was given.

After my heart attack, I became obsessed with the heart. I started reading a book called *Heart: A History* by Dr. Sandeep Jauhar. I was intrigued by all the descriptors we have for the heart. You can have a "big heart," a "small heart," a "cold heart," or a "warm heart." You can learn things "by heart," you can "lead by heart." Some people believe that the soul actually resides in the heart. The heart is intimately connected to our emotions. You can die from a broken heart. You can even die from extreme happiness, at a surprise party, or wedding. Ironically, you can die from public speaking. When these emotionally laden situations stress the heart, the heart weakens. In the area where the heart weakens, it balloons out and this ballooning is called takotsubo cardiomyopathy, or broken heart syndrome. According to Dr. Jauhar, a different part of the heart is involved depending on the emotion. If you end up with broken heart syndrome because of grief, it's the apex of the heart that balloons out. If you have broken heart syndrome from extreme happiness, it's the middle portion of the heart that balloons out. Reading about this made me wonder: Does the heart have a mind of its own?

Let me tell you about my journey. I'm a Kittitian, which means I was born on the island of St. Kitts. My mother is from Dominica, a French Caribbean island, and my father is from Guyana (at the time it was British Guyana), in South America. I left St. Kitts with my family to move to Guyana when I was eighteen months old.

I have fond memories of Guyana, where I lived until I was six. I had a best friend called Natalie. Natalie and I climbed the guava tree in my backyard and picked ripe guavas and ate them. We baked mudpies together and let them harden till they were crisp in the sun. We shared our mud delights and drank invisible tea with our pinkies up—we were "British."

I lived in a house where I could see the Demerara River from my living room window. I saw boats and ferries pass by. I had a pet chicken named Blackie. She was my favorite; she was round and plump. My father took me on his bicycle to school every day through dusty roads where cows and chickens roamed free.

In Guyana, girls and boys wore uniforms to school. We

sang songs in the schoolyard at recess. One of my favorite songs was "Brown Girl in the Ring."

"There's a brown girl in the ring, tra-la-la-la-la. She looks like a sugar in a plum. Plum, plum."

As we sang, we formed a circle around one of the girls. We were all brown girls, but only one girl was in the middle of the circle. We'd say: "Show me your motion, tra-la-la-la-la!" as we watched her hips sway.

We were proud to be brown girls. We were happy brown girls. We celebrated our brownness by singing and dancing: it was beautiful to be brown.

When my mother and I came to the United States, I don't remember grieving the loss of friends and family I left behind. I left a piece of my heart in Guyana when we moved to Queens, New York. I was only six years old, and the year was nineteen sixty-five.

I remember our neighborhood had manicured lawns that were green and lush. I remember the morning dew on the grass formed tiny droplets that moistened my bare feet when I ran across it. There were brick Tudor homes lined up in neat rows with stained-glass windows. There were no more songs about brown girls, and there were no more celebrations of brownness. I learned that in the eyes of white people, being brown wasn't a good thing. Like when our neighbor Evan called me the N-word as I was passing by his house. I didn't know what the N-word meant—I was eight years old, and I was new to this country. I could tell that it wasn't something very nice. It would be years before I understood the depth of its meaning. Another time, Shelley didn't invite me to her birthday party. We used to play stickball and ride our bikes together almost daily. "Shelley, why didn't you invite me to your party?" I asked.

"Well, Hisla, I couldn't possibly invite you to my party because you'd be the only Black person there," she said.

I was ten when that happened, and I remember it like it was yesterday.

When I felt sad, I would ride my bike for hours and think about rides with my father in Guyana. I remembered I sat on the bar of the bicycle between his muscular arms as we rode to school. There were times in that neighborhood in Queens when I needed to be alone, and I would go up the stairs to the top floor of our house. There were stained-glass windows that were angled at forty-five degrees, with a small triangular ledge I could sit on. I would sit on the ledge and open both windows. I looked down the street over treetops and made believe it was my castle with my kingdom below.

There were days in that suburban neighborhood that were idyllic, but the neighborhood was changing. I had no idea what it meant when the white neighbors all started moving away. I didn't know about redlining and white flight. The extended family we had been living with in Queens decided to move to upstate New York. When my mother told me she and I were moving to the Northeast Bronx, I cried. I was scared. I had heard that the Bronx was dangerous. All I knew from watching the news was that there were brown people who were criminals, and many of them seemed to be from the Bronx. The media had instilled in me images of brown people as bad.

When I moved to the Bronx, I realized it wasn't a bad place. The people were just people—hardworking people with families. And there was a mix of brown and white people. I was a little nerdy and I was still playing with Barbies at twelve. I quickly learned when you live in the Bronx, you don't play with Barbies. I learned about other things. I excelled academically, and I was placed in a Special Progress class, so I skipped the eighth grade.

After graduating from high school in the Bronx, I went to Parsons School of Design and graduated with a bachelor of fine arts in fashion design. I worked as a fashion designer, and I moved to a studio apartment in the Chelsea neighborhood of Manhattan. As a designer, I traveled to Hong Kong, Taiwan, Korea, London, Paris, Rome, Milan, and all over Europe. Whenever I arrived home to JFK airport in New York, I would have to line up with the foreigners. I had a green card and a British passport but I felt American. Finally, at the age of twenty-four, I decided to apply for citizenship.

The year was 1984, and there was a lot of racial unrest in New York, so I had some reservations. There was the death of Eleanor Bumpurs, an elderly woman with a mental health disability. When the police came to give her an eviction notice, she ended up dead, shot twice in her home in New York. I was still shaken up by the death of other Black and brown people in New York including Michael Stewart, who died in police custody. He was an art student suspected of writing graffiti in the subway. He was beaten, and twenty-seven students from the Parsons School of Design heard him screaming "What did I do? What did I do?"

In my Chelsea neighborhood, I watched as police officers straddled and repeatedly punched a young man, as his girlfriend and child were screaming: "Please stop, don't beat him." Then they got tired of hearing the girlfriend screaming so they grabbed her, and the child was left alone, and she said, "Please, my child." I was in a crowd of people watching this, and I screamed, "Please, stop beating him! Why are you hitting him?" And the police officer turned and looked at me and said, "Just shut the fuck up, or you will be next." I ran home, and I cried. I cried because I didn't know if I wanted to belong to a country that didn't want me. I cried because I didn't know what to do, or who to call. I cried because I realized my life could change in an instant and I would have no one to help me.

Despite the horrible things that were happening in the city, I loved New York. I loved New York for the ethnic diversity. I had wonderful friends from all over the world, who were architects and designers, historians and philosophers. Chelsea and the fashion scene was booming. There were fantastic museums and great nightclubs like Danceteria, Area, and the Pyramid. I was welcomed in all the clubs and I had a great time. I loved biking through the streets and weaving through traffic, like a messenger. New York was beautiful even with all the dirt and grime. I loved it.

I became an American citizen and decided to pursue my childhood dream and apply to medical school. I had always wanted to be a doctor, and my mother was supportive of my dreams. My mother had left Guyana, a country she loved, and the husband she loved for the sake of my future and our future generations. I think that's the story of most immigrants—they leave their home and places they love, they leave family members behind, and that doesn't make sense to a lot of people. They do it because they want a better future for their children and grandchildren. My mother remained in the United States from the day she landed and had planned to return to Guyana to be with my father when she retired. In 1987, my father died before she could return to see him, and within a few weeks of his passing, she developed congestive heart failure. My mother died within a year, and in retrospect I believe it was likely she died of broken heart syndrome (the condition was not scientifically described until after her passing).

I was twenty-eight, both my parents were gone, and it felt like the foundation had been wiped out from under my feet. My roots were gone, my home was gone. I didn't know where I belonged.

Three weeks after I buried my mother, I started medical school. Although she had suffered a stroke and couldn't communicate before she died, she had a moment of lucidity the last time I saw her, and we were able to say goodbye. I don't remember having time to grieve. I started medical school with the determination that nothing would stop me from succeeding, not even my mother's passing. I dedicated myself to other people's healing without regard for my own need to heal.

Flash forward, to July 2015. I live in Boston, and I'm visiting Philly for the July 4th weekend. I have a spontaneous coronary artery dissection—a rare heart attack. I suspect it's the result of pushing away decades of grief, loss, and stress into a dark void. On the day of my SCAD, I prayed. I prayed and I prayed and I prayed that I would live. On that day, I made a promise to myself that, if I survived, I was going to make changes in my life. I realized my heart was speaking to me and I needed to listen and to feel. My heart told me: *You need to be some place where people love you. You need to be some place where you can reconnect with them—not just say a quick hello on Facebook or send a text. You need to quit your rat-race job. You need to leave that loveless relationship, because it's depleting you.*

I moved from Boston back to New York, the city I love. I ended my relationship and I quit my rat-race job. Finally, my heart is at home. It took a heart attack to open the doors of my heart and let the light in. It took a heart attack for me to listen. We all have hearts that sing to us regardless of where we come from. Remember to listen for your heart's song when it calls you home.

———————

DR. HISLA BATES, MD, was born on the island of St. Kitts and Nevis and lived in Guyana, South America, before coming to the United States. She is a Parsons School of Design graduate, and fashion designer, who changed careers to follow her childhood dream of becoming a physician. She continues to have a passion for the arts and is a printmaker, painter, illustrator, and writer who is working on her memoir. She is a graduate of the State University of New York, University at Buffalo School of Medicine and Biomedical Sciences, with medical residencies at Harvard Medical School, Mount Sinai School of Medicine, and Yale Medical School. Hisla is a psychiatrist and physician coach in private practice in New York City, who integrates the creative arts in mental health healing.

Birth

BY SOFIJA STEFANOVIC

I gave birth in a New York hospital last month. I don't love new experiences, so the idea of producing a human from my own body, in a city where I don't know many people, in a hospital system I'd watched scary documentaries about was not something I was thrilled about.

When I was a kid in the Australian suburbs at a sleepover, I'd work myself into a state, pretend to feel unwell, call my mother, and tell her in Serbian that I wanted to go home. I'd leave my friends to the Australian things that freaked me out: coleslaw with sweet mayo, beds with top sheets, parents who drank beer and played charades (instead of watching *SBS World News* and cursing about the war back home like my parents). I'd get back to our apartment, which had proper cabbage salad (cabbage, vinegar, oil, salt), ashtrays full of butts from cigarettes smoked indoors, the topless portrait of my aunt that my mother displayed in the living room—things so comforting, I'd go to bed as if my pillow was a cloud under my face, delighted to not be in Lisa's bedroom eating Caramello Koala chocolates.

As my due date neared, I wanted to make that pick-me-up call to my mother. Here in New York, unfamiliar things abounded—a health-care system loaded with hidden costs; my own body's changes; my partner, Michael, who is Australian, politely rejecting my baby name suggestions and looking concerned when I'd blast my Yugo rock playlist, songs from the era before the wars, when Yugoslavia was still intact.

Where was I hoping that playlist would take me anyway? For one thing Yugoslavia doesn't exist anymore. And even when it did, when my mother gave birth to me, she had to share a bed with another woman whose calloused heels scratched her under the sheets. It's not like I longed for that experience.

No, as my due date neared, if there was any place I wanted to be transported to, it was to my bed when I was a preteen, when I had no responsibilities—let alone a soon-to-be child of my own—and I could stay up as late as I wanted reading a book, knowing my parents and little sister were shouting-distance away.

So what happened in the end, then? I gave birth in a New York hospital and now I stand before you, a month later. Sure, I didn't have to share a bed with anyone's scratchy feet, but at least the health care in Yugoslavia was free. It's not like the 50K my insurance was billed got me a cocktail after my thirty-six-hour labor, or cable, or sanitary pads actually. When it was time to push, the doctor who delivered my baby told me I was lazy and that she had two others waiting, and then she talked to the nurses about how she was going shoe shopping that afternoon as I screamed, and when my son was finally born, she botched my stitches so that they came undone a week later and I still have an open wound because it has to heal by itself, because restitching would risk infection. I didn't curse her then, but maybe it's something we can do together now: let us wish that her new shoes blister her terribly—so terribly, it causes a tear in her vagina that has to heal on its own. But I digress.

Back to the recovery room. I found myself at another sleepover in a strange place. I looked at my little baby and tried to remember the things that soothed me, memories from when I was little in Belgrade, before we emigrated. The smell of coffee with grounds that my grandma searched for the future in, cheesy pastries adopted during Ottoman times that can be found in every Belgrade bakery, the perfume my mother wore when she was young. What would my little son's first memories be, being a baby in New York? Trash? Rats? Sirens? Would I pass on my culture to him, or would I cower? I remembered a hot summer in Melbourne, when my five-year-old sister found me in the playground and complained in Serbian about being lonely on her first day of school. The other girls told me I had to speak in English, and to my sister's confusion, I did. Why had I been so easily chastised then? Why had I never played Yugo rock to Michael? Could I turn it all around, by speaking to my baby in my language and gaining a coconspirator, someone to talk to about Michael behind his back? Or would my son roll his eyes at me and, like those girls, tell me to speak in English, my culture disappearing just like that?

At that moment, one of the nurses wheeled in the woman who I was to share the recovery room with. She was woozy after a C-section and spoke with an accent. As the nurse helped her into bed, she asked the woman where she was from, and the woman answered "ex-Yugoslavia." From her name, I worked out that her people and mine were on opposite sides of the war that scattered us across the globe. Neither of us mentioned it. She offered me some Smoki, puffed peanut snacks Yugos grew up on, which she'd got from a deli in Queens. But I already had my own Smoki, which I'd ordered online from a wholesaler that profited off Yugo-nostalgics by selling the low-quality products of our childhood at marked-up prices. We opened the curtain separating our beds and put our babies' bassinets next to each other as we munched on our snacks.

I want to say that this night in the hospital, with my new baby and someone who was also raised on the smell of black coffee and Marlboro cigarettes, was the best sleepover. I want to say that I played my Yugo rock playlist and that my neighbor and I sang along to it together. That we lit up a couple of cigarettes and talked about everything—our country as it was when "Brotherhood and Unity" was the slogan, that we cursed the wars, that we discussed being immigrants in New York. I want to say that I shared my hormonally charged concerns with her: that I asked if she was also worried she'd pass on certain fears to her little one, epigenetically, like that study that found if mother mice were scared by something—if they got a zap to the foot and it was accompanied by an odor—their babies would be scared by the odor, even though they weren't getting zapped.

But we didn't talk about any of that. Instead, we lay there with our new wounds, as our babies slept or cried, and we talked about how cute they were, and I forgot for a little while all the things that were bothering me. When the nurse came into the hospital room that smelled of peanutty childhoods far away, when she heard us talking in another language and saw the open curtain, she said, "Well, everyone's gotten pretty friendly in here!" and she was right.

———————

SOFIJA STEFANOVIC is the creator and host of This Alien Nation, a celebration of immigration. Her memoir, *Miss Ex-Yugoslavia*, is a sometimes funny sometimes dark story about being an immigrant kid during the Yugoslavian Wars. She's a regular storyteller with the Moth and has traveled with their Mainstage, telling personal stories across the country. Her writing has appeared in publications such as the *New York Times*, among others.

4

Attachments

A visiting Korean uncle almost scares himself to death;
a daughter recounts decades of unwanted fashion advice;
friction forms between a mother and daughter on Staten Island;
a writer wrestles with her first and second languages and the
unique powers they hold; an "ungrateful" child looks back

Stories by Alexander Chee, Alice Pung,
Roxanne Fequiere, Maria Tumarkin,
and Mashuq Mushtaq Deen

The Heart Attack Uncle

BY ALEXANDER CHEE

One summer in the early aughts, my uncle Bill arrived to New York City from Seoul, South Korea, to campaign to become a member of the ILC, the International Law Commission at the UN. When I met up with him at his Koreatown hotel, the one he always stayed at while visiting New York, he told me he would be—if he was elected—the first Korean member ever. He was first incredibly excited about this and soon also very worried about it. And as we ate he seemed to alternate between the two emotions.

He repeated what he said whenever he saw me: that me, my brother, and my sister were like his children, as his younger brother, my father, had been very close to him. My father had died when I was fifteen years old and Uncle Bill was the first to reassure us that he would be there for us out of all the members of our father's family. My father and he had been the first of their family to move to America, but he, unlike my dad, had moved back to Korea.

He was dressed as always in his elegant uniform that never varied: khaki pants, tasseled loafers, chambray shirt, paisley ascot, navy blue button-down blazer with brass buttons or gold ones, and a London Fog overcoat. He usually added a beret if it was cold and a tasseled Burberry scarf. By the first time I remember seeing him dressed this way, he had graduated from Georgetown law, given up his career at the University of Virginia, and given up on becoming an American, after his father ordered him to come home to Seoul sometime in the late 1960s. He became a respected legal scholar there, taught at universities in Seoul, and advised several of Korea's presidents on international treaty law, his specialty. He arrived to this campaign in New York that week as a divorced single man living alone in Seoul, and this work was the work of his life. We used to laugh at his uniform but it is now my belief these clothes held him together through all this—something he was in control over that would not change.

He would usually tell me at some point in any visit that he wanted to give it all up, move back to the US and open up a fish and chips shop. I have no idea why, as he never ate them whenever we were together. The first time he said this I thought he was joking, and he laughed when I laughed, but then he argued the case for what a good life it would be. In any case, he did not mention the chip shop on this visit. This was instead the first time in my life that I'd ever seen him excited about his own career.

I said good night, took the train back to Brooklyn, and the next day, he called me from an emergency room, telling me he thought he was having a heart attack, and had gone to get himself checked out. I raced over from my apartment in the South Slope, meeting him in time for him to be discharged by a weary doctor who had found nothing wrong with him.

He had once actually had a heart attack, and it was true he

could have another one. But five times that week I received these phone calls from him, usually from an emergency room but sometimes from his hotel room, telling me that he thought he was sure he was having a heart attack. I would race in again and he would be, by then, in the company of another doctor who had told him that he was fine. This continued all through the week of his campaign, and eventually, after the fifth time, as we went in a taxi back to his hotel, I said to him, "You are an incredibly smart man, you are a brilliant man in fact, and you are so brilliant that you might even scare yourself to death, and so you have to stop."

He nodded in agreement. "You're very precise," he said. "Just like your mother." The calls stopped until he called to tell me he had won his ILC campaign.

. . .

We had a celebratory meal before he left and he told me a story of his visit to the Chinese embassy. The Chinese ambassador had looked at his card and said, "Your last name is Chinese."

And my uncle replied, "Well, yes, but we haven't lived in China for six hundred years."

The Chinese ambassador replied, "Six hundred years is not such a very long time in China. You have our support." This support turned out to be key to his winning this position on the law commission.

We are part of that group of Koreans who have Chinese ancestry, something I've had to explain in various less graceful ways over the years, usually to Chinese people cheerfully insisting to me, "You are Chinese!" to which I have said only, "I sort of am." The way my uncle explained it to me when I was young, our original ancestor, as he is called, was a Mongolian general who married a Korean princess as a part of uniting Korea to the Mongolian Empire. This is of course the simplification of history offered by a grown man to a child. But what is apparent to me only now is what it would mean for a Korean legal scholar to be part of the ILC, given the history of Korea in the twentieth century, as a former colony of Japan always in Japan's shadow on the international stage—and given the role the UN had played in the colonization of Korea, as well as in the division of Korea that led to the Korean War. As someone who was born into Japanese colonial rule, who worked steadily on behalf of stateless Koreans abandoned in China, Russia, and Japan after that colonial rule ended at the end of World War II, it wasn't an empty honor to him. His whole life had been shaped by people wielding power like the kind he had just won.

All that talk about a chip shop had been about giving up on himself and this work. About the seeming impossibility of repairing or restoring what was lost. After that week I told the story of him, I came to call him my "Heart Attack Uncle," and I laughed at the story as I told it, thinking it was a story about a man who was smart enough to scare himself to death. Wasn't that ironic? But no, I had it wrong. I was watching him, that week, master his heart at last, after a life of letting other people rule it. Him on a tightrope made out of his life. Sometimes all the answers to the mystery of someone are right in front of you to put together if you're paying attention. I knew he needed what came to him at last. I saw him through. I just wish I could tell him what I see now.

———

ALEXANDER CHEE is the author of the novels *Edinburgh* and *The Queen of the Night*, and the essay collection *How to Write an Autobiographical Novel*, all from Houghton Mifflin Harcourt. He is a contributing editor at the *New Republic*, and an editor at large at *VQR*. His essays and stories have appeared in the *New York Times Magazine*, *T Magazine*, the *Sewanee Review*, the *Yale Review*, and *Guernica*, among others, and are anthologized in the 2016 and 2019 *Best American Essays*. He is the winner of a 2003 Whiting Award, a 2004 NEA Fellowship in prose and a 2010 MCCA Fellowship, the Randy Shilts Prize in gay nonfiction, the Paul Engle Prize, the 2018 *One Story* magazine's Mentor of the Year Award, and residency fellowships from the MacDowell Colony, the VCCA, Civitella Ranieri, and Amtrak. He is an associate professor of English and creative writing at Dartmouth College.

Three Decades of Unsolicited Fashion Advice from a Migrant Mother

BY ALICE PUNG

This piece was performed in Melbourne, Australia, May 2018

1988—I Am Seven

There is nothing wrong with your father dressing up in his best suit to get two dollars' of milk from Sims Tuckerbag grocery store. What do you mean it's embarrassing? It's dignified. Look at how dignified he is. He looks like he's on important business.

Stop laughing at his shoes. Sometimes it's too cold to wear flip-flops and too hot to wear shoes. So what, "flip-flops with socks"! Well, if it's good enough for the Japanese Crown Prince, it's good enough for us.

You're always going on about footwear. Just last week, you wouldn't wear that beautiful dress I got you for Kelly's party at McDonald's. There was nothing wrong with it! Looked exactly like Princess Diana's wedding gown, but shorter and purpler. Even an improvement, because it had all those little ribbon roses on the neckline. "Oh, I can't wear that with runners!" you cried. What's wrong with runners? Runners are clean, and white, and go well with frilly socks. They're your only shoes. You should be grateful. Truly. Do you know how many girls back in Cambodia can only dream of such an outfit? Did you know, back in Cambodia children are spreading poisonous glue onto the soles of these sneakers with their bare hands! Your uncle visited a factory, he saw with his own eyes.

Oh, here's your dad coming back now. Yes, yes, I realize now that no one else down the street dresses like this. But they are hooligans who'll never leave the Alcan Trailer factory. Yes, yes, I know your dad also worked there. But at least he looks like an educated Singaporean instead of a skin-and-bones refugee, so skinny that if he turned around sideways he would disappear from view. No, truly, did you know when your dad was surviving those Killing Fields of Cambodia, he was so thin that if he breathed inward, you could feel his backbone through his stomach?

You kids don't know what it's like to starve.

1998—I Am Seventeen

I thought you liked it! Scalloped white lace. Sleeves. I got it from Myer! Sure it was on sale, but come on, it's from a department store! I don't own anything from Myer. Your teachers at the valedictory dinner tonight said you looked lovely. No, they weren't just being nice. Even your friend Fatima's mum asked me where I got it from. See, I was nice,

I didn't tell her that there would be none left that would fit her daughter.

What's that? Where does it say that it's for a twelve-year-old? What's a confirmation dress? Well, how was I supposed to know? You know I can't read. It's a beautiful dress. Stop sulking in the back of the car. Don't think I can't see you in the rearview mirror.

You wanted to dress like the other girls? Did you see how short their skirts were? Did you see how tight their tops were? Some of them look as if they were scooped into their outfits with shoehorns. Let me tell you something: A girl is like cotton wool. Once she's dirtied she can never be clean again. A boy is like a gem, the more you polish it, the brighter it shines. It doesn't matter how dirty a boy gets—they always come out on top. Why is that sexy? Oh, you said *sexist*. I don't know what that means, you know my English isn't too good.

2008—I Am Twenty-Seven

You know you don't have to spend a lot of money to look good. Look at those *Vogue* magazines you waste money on. Do any of those models look happy? Of course not. They're wearing crap like fried eggs on their chests and broccoli hats, but they look like they haven't had food in five years, let alone fiber.

Now look at this Target ad—look how happy this girl is wearing her twenty-five-dollar polyester wrap dress. Good skin, good hair, lots of leftover notes in her wallet for a twelve-dollar pair of jeggings even.

And look at this Best and Less catalog. See that kid? He's only four but he knows a bargain when he sees one. He's almost pissing himself in excitement because of his Spiderman socks. And look at his mum, smiling in her twelve-dollar bra and four-dollar lace panties.

See, the better the bargain, the happier the wearer.

2018—I Am Thirty-Seven

Why'd you take the tie off him? I know he's only three years old. What do you mean he looks like a miniature accountant? You think that's a bad thing? What's wrong with dreaming big? Oh, oh, so you think it's boring. Is that it? The worst thing that can ever happen to you in your office job is you suffer from a paper cut, and that is boring is it? Ling lost his three fingers to the meat cleaver at the restaurant! I worked with potassium cyanide for ten years in that back garage making all that jewelry.

You want to layer your son in clothes like those white kids? T-shirts over shirts and shorts over leggings sort of thing? Rainbow socks that don't match? Let me tell you something. White kids can do that and look cute and quirky, you dress your little Asian boy that way and he looks povvo and fresh off the boat! What the hell? I know those raggy Oishi-m shorts with the ghost patch on the bum cost $44. I saw them at Highpoint Shopping Centre. Your auntie could sew him a pair with the Country Road offcuts she keeps from her back-garage sewing days.

You have no idea. People judge. In ten years' time they'll think he'll be shoplifting in Kmart. Why do you think those private schools dress their boys in little woolen suits? So people will start respecting them when they're five years old!

Anyhow, Wednesday is my day to look after him, and if you don't like the way I dress him you can put him in child-care for a hundred and thirty dollars a day.

You still want me to look after him?

Good.

Hey, you're back from work early. Let me tell you something that happened today.

I was at the Medicare office this afternoon. There was an African lady and her husband in front of me. The man reminded me of your father. I knew he dressed up in his best suit to go to Highpoint. She was another matter. You know what she was wearing? A floor-length bright red ball gown with a matching bolero! It had sequins and diamantes on it! In the middle of the day. I know what you'd say about this—tacky. But she stood very straight. The two of them looked like they came out of the television, like royalty, like Oprah & Friends. (Why is that racist? She's beautiful and a millionaire.)

People were staring at them, but I know they were jealous.

I couldn't help myself. "You beautiful," I said.

She winked at me. "Savers secondhand store."

You see, what you call "good taste" is for those with too much money and no imagination. What that lady wore was true style, movie star glory.

Hey, I know you got those Oishi-m shorts for him in Savers. Good on you. I know because I went there after Medicare Oprah told me about it. I saw another pair, here, I got them for you.

Those shorts look crap, but at least you didn't pay fifty bucks for something that looks secondhand even when new.

But remember—never tell your aunties that you dress your son in secondhand clothes.

People judge.

———

ALICE PUNG is an award-winning Australian author whose books include *Unpolished Gem*, *Her Father's Daughter*, *Lucy and Linh*, and *Growing up Asian in Australia*. She was named after Lewis Carroll's creation because when her father arrived in Australia from the Killing Fields of Cambodia, he thought their new country was a Wonderland.

An Island Unto Herself

BY ROXANNE FEQUIERE

The problem wasn't what my brother said, but rather where he said it. Exposed beneath the harsh lights of an A&P checkout lane, he'd made a motion toward some candy an arm's length from the shopping cart where he sat and asked my mother if he might have some. Her attention was elsewhere, so he called to her by her name—not Mom or Mama, but her given name, Marie. My brother was only repeating the name he'd heard his parents use at home; they hadn't bothered to call each other "Mom" and "Dad," and so neither did their child.

At this point in the story, the way my mother tells it, she pauses for effect, cringing to illustrate her decades-old discomfort. "Now all these white people are looking at me funny, wondering whose child I'm shopping with," she says, the sharp edge in her voice belying the smile on her face. It's a story that neatly encapsulates the casual comedy of moving through the world with a young child in tow, but it's clear that the memory of those strange looks still stings after all those years. When they got home, she told her toddler—

gently, but in no uncertain terms—that he really ought to start calling her Mommy.

I believe this anecdote took place during the early '80s, a few years after my parents had gotten married and moved from Brooklyn's Prospect Heights to Staten Island. By their account, the decision was a logistical one. My mother, one of six children, wanted six of her own. (In the end, she had three.) On Staten Island she could have a whole house in which to raise them, instead of the cramped apartment she and her family had crammed themselves into upon arriving in Brooklyn from Haiti years earlier. Long before overpopulation clogged the Staten Island Expressway and crowded its schools, my mother recalls the island's abundance of open space with a touch of wonder. Here was a place where she could, at long last, spread out a bit.

. . .

In Prospect Heights, my mother's family had played a central role in establishing a bustling community of Haitian immigrants. My grandmother launched a Girl Scout troop led by my mother and installed a local chapter of her beloved church group at St. Teresa of Avila next door. The girls gathered at the family apartment to try their hand at cooking griot and banan peze. On Sundays after Mass, drummers lined the wall of the church's basement rec room, a group of barefoot girls gathered in the center to learn Haitian dance.

On Staten Island, my mother was cut off from this cultural camaraderie. What she had was "all these white people": eyeing her in the grocery store, frowning at the sound of her accent, making snide comments. The demographics were stacked against her; it was all she could do not to make waves.

She took those awkward moments in which her otherness was amplified and turned them into teachable ones. Her sister's firstborn hadn't spoken any English when she first enrolled in school—only Haitian Kreyol, the language she'd heard and spoken exclusively at home. It wasn't that her parents couldn't speak English—it simply hadn't occurred to them to speak it in private, away from American ears. That wasn't a mistake my mother was about to make. At home, Kreyol was for my parents; my brothers and I spoke only English.

I should pause here and clarify. My mother was and is fiercely proud of her home country and heritage. She could be a harshly astute observer of our neighbors' ignorance. Watching her march into my school to raise hell over some classmate's racist slight or other was a sight to behold. She encouraged her children to be equally proud of our roots, and to express it by pursuing excellence at all costs. The way she saw it, we lived on an island where we'd always stand out by default—it was our responsibility to do right by those we represented; to not live down to any negative stereotypes. Of course, it's difficult to define yourself by the spaces you don't occupy.

As a kid, I found it relatively easy to fulfill my mother's requirements for success. I pulled straight As, read voraciously, and carried myself well. Beyond the classroom, though, I railed against what felt like her endless machinations to tether me to the house. When my peers made friendly overtures, extending invitations to after-school hangouts, my mother crinkled her nose. "I'll never understand this American habit, sending your children over to some stranger's home," she said. "I don't even know these people." Eager to accommodate, I'd offer to arrange an impromptu mom meeting at school, or maybe an introductory phone call. Without fail, she'd refuse, those old insecurities about her accent or some other immigrant identifier flaring up again.

It was a routine that drove me crazy. *Your English is fine*, I told her. *Am I supposed to never make friends?* I asked her. *You talk about Americans as if I'm not American*, I said to her. That one usually sparked a long, fiery lecture—yes, I was American by birth, but all throughout my life, people would try and make me feel otherwise. I'd learn that soon enough, she'd respond. *Okay, but that has nothing to do with the fact that you never let me out of the house*, I threw back at her.

Over time, my mother was shrinking and folding in on herself, taking refuge in her own home to avoid the scrutiny of those who might ridicule her, but my adolescent appraisal of the situation was that she was just trying to thwart my attempts at a social life. It would be years before I could see her side of the argument with any empathy.

In the meantime, we bickered endlessly. I measured my success in this endeavor by how far I could get from my house and for how long: an early school day followed by multiple extracurriculars (a few miles away, nine hours); an after-school job (a few more miles away, ten hours a week); a school trip to Disney World that I'd organized myself and therefore couldn't miss (1,110 miles away, four days); a college degree (230 miles away, four years); a tiny apartment shared with friends in the East Village (20 miles away, indefinitely).

One day, I realized I no longer needed to negotiate and wrangle time away from home. The dutiful daughter within, forever at war with the independent woman I wanted to be, I always called my mother at takeoff and touchdown, whether traveling for business or pleasure, but it slowly dawned on me that these were calls of courtesy. I could go exploring for the hell of it, and I didn't need to loop anyone else in on my plans unless I wanted to. My thoughts drifted to Paris, where I'd been once before for a study abroad program. I realized that I could go there—and everywhere else—on my own terms.

I was in the middle of drawing up a plan for a three-month European tour when the idea of inviting my mother along occurred to me. She'd been moored on Staten Island for so long, working hard to provide for my family. Maybe all her professed disdain for adventures outside the home had simply been a defense mechanism. After all, balancing a marriage, family, and backbreaking work as a special needs caregiver probably didn't leave much time for dreams of far-flung voyages. Here was a chance for both of us to get away, to experience the feeling of being foreign in tandem for once, without all the excess baggage. Here was a chance for me to show her what the freedom I'd been battling her to claim for so long looked like.

I called her up and rattled off the seven countries I was planning to visit. She could choose the country she wanted to see most, I told her, and I could arrange for her to fly out and meet me. She politely declined, as casually as if I'd invited her to a Sunday matinee. I repeated my offer, this time with more detail. Surely she hadn't grasped the magnitude of my proposal? She declined again. And again. It wasn't long before we'd assumed our usual roles: me, pleading on behalf of some new experience; my mother, digging her heels in and refusing. Her responses grew clipped. I couldn't coax any reasoning out of her, but it seemed to me that after so many years, my mother still felt like a foreigner in her chosen home. She had no desire to travel abroad and feel similarly.

I went on without her—to Edinburgh, Florence, and Oslo, where it seemed as though every one of our immigrant cab-drivers had a story about a scholarship in the States they'd turned down for Norway's superior quality of life; to Geneva, Barcelona, and Marseille, where our waiter looked at my Korean friend and me and guessed that we were from New York, because, in his words, we looked like a Benetton ad, and where else in the world could we have struck up a friendship?

Years later, in Athens, where few people looked like me, a jeweler commented on how gold looks wonderful on my dark skin—I chose to take the compliment. In Havana, women with complexions like mine smiled at me and assumed our shared heritage before I told them, in rusty high school level Spanish, that my people hail from another Caribbean island. In Indonesia, I stuck out like a sore thumb and made a conscious decision to ignore the several looks cast my way. As I continue to make my way through and around the world, there have been painful clashes and moments of ridicule alongside laughter and snippets of enlightenment, but I'm still exploring, wandering far from home and then tracing my way back. It's a habit that took shape as a form of rebellion, but has since become a powerful method of introspection. As it turns out, I can't define myself by the spaces I don't occupy.

ROXANNE FEQUIERE is a multidisciplinary writer based in New York City. She's written for publications including the *New York Times*, *Vogue*, the *Village Voice*, and *ELLE* and crafted copy for clients ranging from the New York City Mayor's Office to Nike. She might just make it after all.

Second Language

BY MARIA TUMARKIN

This piece was performed in Melbourne, Australia, May 2018

In English I can say "I love you" to a man in a month or two. Not just to any man, don't worry, to a man I am with. The words fall out of my mouth like milk teeth. "I love you." "I hate you." God is not listening when I speak English.

In Russian, my birth language, it would take years of not saying it to say "I love you." In Russian the word *love* (*lyubov*) and the word *freedom* (*svoboda*) sometimes have a crushing weight. Just to lift them up to my mouth takes most of my strength.

We are chained to words in our birth languages.

In English I am free.

A birth language is vulgar, hot, world-making, capable of slicing and splicing like a battle-ready samurai katana sword. When it's beautiful—and it's frequently beautiful—it's, by itself, a reason to live. When it's degraded—and it's frequently degraded, at least where I come from—it makes the world feel precarious, on the verge of being trashed.

A second, third language is a code. A system. You pick it like a lock. At the beginning at least, it cannot evoke or injure beyond the superficial. You speak a new language with your mouth. You write it with your hand as if driving a tractor.

I read somewhere, in some learned multiauthor investigation, that bilingual speakers report decreased levels of anxiety and arousal when they come across sexual references or obscenities in their second language. No blushing, no getting horny.

We do not choose our parents. We do not choose the language our family flees toward.

I come to Australia as I am about to turn sixteen. My English is, at first, virtually nonexistent, then—simply shit. I declare, "Thank you for your hostility." I mean, "Thank you for your hospitality." It takes me two hours to enroll in a local library. Who is torturing who? Me with cement in my mouth or that librarian who can't for the life of him understand what I am telling him?

English is out to defeat me. I am a Lilliputian in the land of Gullivers. An underperforming lab rat lost in a maze, running out of my rat juice.

And it's like that every time I step out of the house. Trains, trams, Department of Social Security, shops, banks, Medicare, a rowing club on the banks of Yarra I join (which is funny because I can't even swim and because in a couple of months I'll fracture my arm while training. A native speaker is addressing me in English and I am concentrating so hard, working so hard to understand him, I put my arm behind my seat on a rowing machine and ride over it.)

When my fractured arm heals, when I get better at hostility and hospitality, when I get proficient—that's the inelegant word for it, isn't it?—it becomes clear to me that I can't be a writer in English. Becoming a writer was my plan since the age of seven but immigration had killed that one off. Yes, yes, bring up Nabokov now. Or Brodsky. Or another Joseph—Conrad, who also conquered English. Or Bosnian Aleksandar Hemon. Or Polish Eva Hoffman. Or Pakistani Mohsin Hamid. Or Mexican Valeria Luiselli.

I am not them.

Eva Hoffman was a teenager, too, when her family immigrated to Canada from Poland. In her book *Lost in Translation: A Life in a New Language*, she remembers coming across the word *river* in English and finding it cold, dry, unflowing, flat. A word without an aura. "'River' in Polish," Hoffman writes, "was a vital sound, energized with the essence of riverhood, of my rivers, of my being immersed in rivers. 'River' in English . . . has no accumulated associations for me . . . it does not give off the radiating haze of connotation."

The words you learn in the new language are cold and hollow at first, and the new world around you is like that, too—no aura, little pulse.

What happens then? You know what happens then.

Slowly, slowly, the word *river* in the new language starts swelling, extending into the third dimension, setting off a memory of smells and sensations; slowly, slowly, it becomes fuller, more intimate, more sentient, magnetized with meaning, and when one day you find yourself saying in your new language, to your children perhaps, the words of Heraclitus, "No man ever steps in the same river twice," the word *river* might just feel big enough, deep enough, too, to stand in for time and its passing.

In Russian I am in a valley surrounded by tall mountains—the day's clear, the visibility's second to none. I am on notice for every moment of smugness, of overplaying my hand or obfuscating. God help me (she won't) if I take myself too seriously and my subject matter not seriously enough.

English is for school assignments and undergraduate essays and my honors thesis on the history of sleep and my PhD on physical sites of trauma; it is for emails to electricity providers (subject line: Request for a payment extension) and to my daughter's school principal that time when she was shamed in front of her class for playing the game in which whoever said the word *penis* the loudest won and she won and was then made by her teacher, a middle-aged man, his face burning, to write the word *penis* on the whiteboard many times over to put the fear of God into her or something, whatever was the plan, it succeeded for a while there, she was eleven. In that email to a suburban school principal I brought up Joseph Stalin and the show trials. Moscow of 1930s. Totalitarianism starts small, I said. Not a problem. I was writing in English.

The word *hybridity* feels too domesticated, beige. *Multicultural* is even worse. It smells like a UNESCO brochure. *Bicultural* is okay, I guess. Tricultural. A statement of fact. Chilean American writer Ariel Dorfman talks about the bicultural fate as marked by "incessant and often perverse doubleness."

Second, third language is not something you stick a flag in. What you want from it is not to yield to you, to drop its defenses, but to hold you in its thrall and its line of vision. What you want is not mastery, but—that's the inelegant word for it, isn't it?—accountability.

"To have a second language is to possess a second soul" is an old saying you would have heard. Have you heard the one about a second face? Italian writer and linguist Diego Marani says that our face "is shaped by the muscles we move to pronounce the sounds of our language."

When did it happen? I can't tell you. Somehow I stopped

writing in Russian, started writing in English. What I can tell you is that I no longer spit the word *love* or the word *home* or the word *freedom* out at will like kids and old women used to spit out chewed sunflower seeds in my childhood. These words are soaked in life, in other people's lives; they have a visceral, spoon-bending power. English has moved deep into me. I cannot sell my children down the river in it. It counts. It sticks. I will burn for all the false, empty words I've written in it. Finally, I will burn.

MARIA TUMARKIN was born in the former Soviet republic of Ukraine and now lives in Melbourne, Australia. She writes books, essays, reviews, and pieces for performance and radio as well as collaborating with sound and visual artists. Tumarkin is the author of four books of ideas. The latest, *Axiomatic*, won the 2018 Melbourne Prize for Literature's Best Writing Award and was named a *New Yorker* Top 10 Book of 2019. Maria is a recipient of the 2020 Windham Campbell Prize in the nonfiction category. She holds a PhD in cultural history and is a senior lecturer in the creative writing program at the University of Melbourne.

Ungrateful

BY MASHUQ MUSHTAQ DEEN

I would like to tell you a story about my parents. I was born here, but my parents are immigrants—and not just immigrants, but people with whom I did not get along for many years.

I never would have described my parents as patient people. They were demanding and strict and they expected the best from my brother and me—the best grades, the best colleges, the best everything. We were the model minority, the stereotype: My brother and I were both valedictorians in our small Connecticut high school. He went on to MIT, Stanford, and Columbia. I went on to Columbia and then dropped out of school and spent a year in a hospital because I was suicidal. Okay, so not exactly the model minority, but it was a totally top-of-the-line hospital—something to definitely brag about if you were the type to brag about your kid being a cutter, and suicidal, and queer, and trans. Which my parents were not.

In hindsight, though, my parents were actually pretty patient people. They were both doctors: my dad was an anesthesiologist, my mom was a pediatrician. They were very educated and very capable people, yet they tolerated their seven-year-old kid—me—correcting their pronunciation of English words, English being the second of three languages they spoke.

They were patient in other ways. When they first emigrated, back in the 1960s, they went from India to England because my father's father wanted him to take the Royal College of Surgeons exams. This is before curry became Britain's national food. They went to England where it seemed like all the food was boiled and bland. There were no Indian grocery stores, no spices, nothing to make anything taste better. Until they discovered ketchup. Ketchup made their food taste like *something* instead of *nothing*.

And my mom, at the age of twenty-five, and my dad, thirty-three, living abroad for the first time, had to live in different cities because that's where the work was, only seeing each other on weekends and holidays. And when my older brother was born, my mom was alone in the hospital because my dad was on a bus trying to get to her.

And then more patience was required. After a few difficult years in England, my parents moved to New York City, where they had to do their residencies all over again because their credentials weren't accepted, and so my dad, who was already a surgeon, now became an anesthesiologist because that was the residency he could find. Residencies back then were even more brutal than they are now—my parents routinely worked thirty-six hours straight in poor conditions. They didn't have much money.

My dad tells a story of when they first moved there: a friend of his, who was also an Indian doctor, went to get his hair cut and the barber told him, "Don't come here, we don't serve niggers here." . . . I didn't know that back then.

I didn't know any of this. I was zero years old. I didn't know that my mom, at the hospital where she worked, was told to "never be alone in the elevator with a man. If he gets on, then you get out." My mother, a young woman from a small village in southern India, had to worry about her physical safety while at work, or when walking home after a long day. She was frightened, but she had to go to work, she had kids to feed, so she did. My brother, only seven years old, had his bike stolen from him while he was still on it—another seven-year-old kid threatened to kill him if he didn't give it up. But I didn't know all that. All I knew in these early years before we moved to the safety of rural Connecticut was that my dad brought home bagels every Saturday, and I ate them with cream cheese while I watched *Tom and Jerry* on TV.

And here's where patient kind of dovetails with generous. Because I certainly would not have—as a naturally self-absorbed teenager—thought of my parents as generous. They were frugal, skimpy, dare I say—a little cheap. I did not get the BB gun that I wanted, I did not get the Jeep Wrangler that I wanted, I did not get an allowance. And though they were both working doctors and I assumed they made good money, they were very secretive about it.

Instead, I was often reminded about poverty. About all the starving kids around the world who were far more deserving than I was. And—it's worth pausing here to emphasize this—we also saw poverty. We went to India every four years to see family and, in the streets, we saw what real, abject poverty looks like. After that, it was hard to take things for granted the way my friends did. It's not like reading about it. And my parents were right—I was not more deserving than those kids were.

Because I did not get everything I wanted and because they saved their pennies and kept the heat too low in winter, I would not have thought my parents to be generous people. But that's because they didn't brag about what they *did* do with their money. To this day, I'm still not sure how many of my cousins they sent to college, how many family members they gave money to, how many surgeries they paid for. I *do* know—and only by chance, because my dad didn't share this with his kids—that he built a school. He built a school! For girls in India to study computers and science, and he named it after his mother. The only reason I found out at all is because one day he was feeling very nervous, and I asked why, and my mother said he had to give a speech at the ribbon-cutting ceremony. And I said, "What ribbon-cutting ceremony?" (He still doesn't talk about it, and he would be appalled that I just told you that.)

Perhaps it's the experience of being an immigrant that breeds patience, or even generosity, I don't know. You can't very well walk around expecting to get whatever you want, whenever you want, when you're the new guy. Or maybe that has more to do with their generation. Or both. But I remember my mom once saying to me that she didn't expect people in this country to understand her culture. Why would they? Of course they asked her questions sometimes. No, she wasn't offended. I sometimes think my friends and I walk around being offended on behalf of our parents, who have no need for our offense. My parents are the type of people who keep their head down and get along. It used to infuriate me. I wanted them to march in Pride Parades, to go to antiwar protests, to do all kinds of things. But it doesn't anymore—infuriate me, I mean.

Sometimes I look back on the things my parents did do.

They were doctors. They saved lives. They lived quietly. They helped people when they could in small and big ways, but always in quiet ways. They raised two children—one who was an ungrateful child. You know, my mom used to say I was "an ungrateful child." She said it with quite a bit of venom when she was really pissed off at me, which was often because I was a soon-to-be queer, transgender artist-type (even if I didn't know it yet), and all those things were terrifying to her. (How can you keep your child safe when they insist on living that kind of life?) And of course, I got defensive and angry and a lot of other things, including a little suicidal. But she was right, because I *was* a child, and so, of course, I was ignorant of all that they did and put up with. Because they were modest and they didn't tell me. Because some things you have to grow up to understand.

I *was* ungrateful and in some ways that was their biggest gift. Their biggest generosity to me was that I didn't know how much had been endured so that I could have this life.

I want to end with a short excerpt of a poem I wrote a few years ago. It's called "Immediate Family" and this is the third and last section called "Translations."

My father slips me a twenty dollar bill when my mother
    isn't looking.
Translation: I care about you.
My mother cooks me my favorite curry and fried chicken
    and then complains about how worn out she is.
Translation: I must love you.
My parents send me a large check in the mail and then
    tell me to invest it in Apple stock so that one day we
    can buy a house.
Translation: I'm sorry?

So many things, never enough. No one ever says "I'm
   sorry."
I'm about to get off the phone with my mom and quickly,
   I say it all in a rush, "byemomIloveyou."
She says "yes, bye, yes, love you too, bye."
Soon they will die and we will never have spoken the same
   language.

MASHUQ MUSHTAQ DEEN is a 2018 Lambda Literary Award win-
ner, and his publications include *Draw the Circle* (Dramatists Play Ser-
vice), *The Betterment Society* (Methuen Books), as well as shorter pieces
in the *Journal of Asian American Studies*, *The Margins* (published by Asian
American Writers' Workshop), and *Plays for Our Younger Selves* (Table
Work Press). His plays have been produced at Rattlestick, Mosaic,
PlayMakers Rep, among other theaters, and include *The Shaking Earth*,
Flood, and *The Empty Place*. He is a company member of New Dra-
matists, a PWC Core Writer, and his work has been supported by the
Sundance Institute/Ucross, Blue Mountain Center, Public Theater,
NYTW, MacDowell, Bogliasco Foundation, Helene Wurlitzer Foun-
dation, and Target Margin Theater, among others. He is represented
by the Gurman Agency. www.mashuqmushtaqdeen.com

5

What Forms Us

An immigrant child's identity is fractured and formed in a new land; an Armenian flees Azerbaijan and finds solace in the Florida Christian rap scene; a Chinese son's return to the motherland does not go as expected; a Mexican girl's American dream is broken on a trip to Disneyland; a stinky elevator serves as a time machine to Warsaw

Stories by Kay Iguh, Rufat Agayev, Agustinus Wibowo, Emma Ramos, and Zuzanna Szadkowski

Mortar, Porcelain, Brick

BY KAY IGUH

1.

Mortar: from the Latin *mortarium*, means crushed.

As a child immigrant, especially when you leave home alone without your entire family, I think your brain breaks, somewhere mid-Atlantic or Pacific or over border lines demarcating here from home, them from us, citizen from alien.

Upon entry, lines on maps rise and become walls. In this new place, you find that one day you are you, and the next, you are not. You don't know who this new person is, and perhaps you're not even interested in finding out. But at a certain point, you must go to school, and at school, teachers and classmates will ask you about yourself. *Which self?* you think. But you know what they mean, so you make up lies. You tell yourself it is for their benefit, so that they can understand without really having to know. You lie about where you were born; instead of naming the town you come from, you name the larger capital city. You lie about who you come from; you say that your parents are dead because it's easier than admitting that your parents are still back home and that you have no idea if you will ever see them again. When they ask for your name, you shorten it to something clean and crisp. When they smile and ask what it means or where it comes from, you smile back and tell them it's made up. But you are no builder. With lies you reduce yourself into plaster, which will be used to bind a new self together. You were never skilled at self-preservation.

As you grow up, you want nothing to do with back home. At least not with the home that everyone else seems to know. You used to think that home is a place where people struggle with one another and struggle with the government, yet they manage to survive. But no, here are textbooks and the BBC telling you that back home is a place where people die of poverty, of illiteracy, where they die simply because they don't know how to live, or perhaps because they don't deserve to live. So you begin to claim places other than home, places like Kenya or Ethiopia, one because it is what everyone thinks of when they think of Africa and the other because it was never colonized. When the astonished parents of your American friends ask, "How are you here?" it is as though they are asking, "Why are you alive?" They can't reconcile the hungry, needy, always dying African they see on TV with the lucid-eyed child before them with the rapidly Americanized accent. You choose pride over injury and choose to believe that they are complimenting your resilience. Your deft masonry. This, too, is a kind of survival—this ability to take everyday insults and spin them into fodder that will fire clay into porcelain.

2.

Porcelain: harder and more durable than all other ceramics, its clay is more refined, desired for its purity.

But the clay of your experience is marked with impurities and complexities. Think of your father and the sands of the Sahara carried by wind to ocean. Think of your mother and southern loam: a mixture of clay, sand, and organic matter from which grows cocoa, rubber, and palm. Think of the alluvial plains of your childhood. Think of mineral-rich water and red rock monoliths.

This, you think, is how a person is made. A composite of geographies and untidy narratives.

Pretty soon, lying becomes so easy that it starts to feel like the real you. You think, maybe this is who I am, or who this new country wants me to be. It is intoxicating, this ability to forge a new self—an entire history—out of scraps of memories and distorted photographs and what you see on TV. Perhaps, you think, this is how to make a future. But in building a future you dismantle a past. In its place is a person hard fought, hard won from an unforgiving country. A person that is worth calling home about—but as you scratch the foil off the calling card to reveal the secret code underneath that will connect you back home, you stop and think: Who do I say is calling?

You justify the lies by saying that you are merely protecting what is precious—the smallest, densest part of you that is still back home with your people. You tell yourself you had locked it away for safekeeping. One day, you try to return to it, to remind yourself of who you are and where you come from, but it's gone. Where did it go? But of course, it had been used for raw material: from mortar to porcelain, and soon, to brick.

3.

Brick: (usually followed by in, up, or over) as in to construct, pave, shore, or wall.

This new country, this land is a kiln that scorches and calcifies clay at desperately high temperatures—sometimes to the point of cracking. It burns so hotly, you wonder, what is it afraid of? For this new self, it is, however, the price of being. Calmly, with your head raised against someone else's fear, you walk into the fire. From mortar to porcelain, you are repurposed into brick. On the other side, you are handed a certificate of congratulations, no longer alien, you have become a countable, usable product. You are a citizen. With your body, this country is fortified. With your body, this country continues.

They lied when they told you that home is lost in miles and time zones and currencies, that it is found in memory. Perhaps they didn't know. Home is lost and found on the tongue when words like *sand* slide down your throat and every time you reach for them, your tongue twists.

Where is the mother tongue from your father-land that will speak life into this crimson body? Where is the language with which you will write yourself, finally, in pen and not in pencil?

Home is tied to the tongue, and tongue to taste, and taste to scent, and scent to memory. Memory, scientists says, is most strongly associated with scent when the smell is of a particularly salient nature—perhaps a moment of transcendent joy followed by "you are going, and we are staying."

The smell of salt water reminds you of home—you have no idea why. You weren't born by the sea, had never seen the ocean, but in dream, a kind of memory, you smell the Pacific or Atlantic, or even the Gulf of Aden, into which parts of you had been shorn. *Home*, you think. *Might I return there to trawl for bits of me at sea?* Ask, how do you pry yourself from the mouths of sharks?

————

KAY IGUH is a fiction writer and educator whose work centers on racial identity and justice. A graduate of the Creative Writing Program at New York University, she has received fellowships from New York State Summer Writers Institute, The Center for Fiction, Vermont Studio Center, and Jack Jones Literary Arts. Her short story "House Girl" won the 2016 Disquiet Literary Prize. Her stories have appeared in *Guernica* and the *LA Review of Books*. A native Nigerian, she grew up in Houston and lives in Brooklyn.

C.R.I.S.I.S.
(Christian Rappers Influenced by Scripture Infiltrating Satan)

BY RUFAT AGAYEV

My name is Rufat. I'm a Caucasian—a real Caucasian. I was born in the Caucasus region of the world, in Baku, Azerbaijan. When you look at me face-to-face, you might think, *That's a regular white guy*, but when you see the profile of my nose you'll say, *Yeah, they don't make those here*. My nose is aerodynamic. It's made for mountainous regions. It's like a spoiler on a sports car, for my face. I have a *Fast and Furious* face. You might see white people perform on this stage tonight, but know: I'm the only actual Caucasian.

In 1992, my mother, father, and I fled a war that was happening between our people, Armenians, and the Azerbaijanis. Fleeing a war sucks, but I like to think of it as something positive. Fleeing is just an advanced form of traveling. We came to the US in 1992 and started a life in Erie, Pennsylvania. Erie was the type of small town that made you want to go back to the war. If you wanted to do something fun in Erie, your choices were either go to the woods or go to the mall. I remember as a kid we'd visit Pittsburgh and my mouth would drop as soon as we entered the city because they had skyscrapers. Not many, but enough for me to feel like I was in New York City. That's the only way I can describe Erie; it makes Pittsburgh feel like the Big Apple.

Starting school wasn't easy for me. My first year in kindergarten, I was in ESL. Two of my friends dared me to keep saying "govno" to the teacher, which means "shit" in Russian. She eventually found out what the word I kept saying meant, and I had to repeat kindergarten. Having to repeat a grade sucked, but not as bad as telling my new American classmates my name and where I was from. As an adult, I struggle to explain where and what Azerbaijan is. Imagine doing that when you're six. Also, a name like Rufat is ripe for remixing. One alteration could be something like . . . I don't know? Rufart. When I would meet new kids outside of school, I would lie and tell them my name was Michael. Moments later they would be like, "Hey, Michael," and I would forget to answer.

As a seven-year-old kid, my first taste of American culture was Shaq. I was mesmerized. I watched his movies (*Steel* and *Kazaam*), bought his rap album (*Shaq Diesel*), played his video game (*Shaq-Fu*), ate his food (the double-decker taco at Taco Bell), and drank his drink (All Sport). I wanted to be Shaq. I wanted to be a seven-foot-two, 325-pound Black man, with a size 22 shoe.

When I was nine, I remember telling my Armenian grandfather that I was planning to become a professional basketball player. He listened, and then sat me down to talk about genetics. He said that Armenians don't have bodies that can handle the rigors of the NBA, and that maybe I should try a sport Armenians are physically built for, like chess. Yeah, he shot down my dream, but looking at it now, he was right. There has never been an Armenian in the National Basketball Association, and there never will be. Even if we were on a team, we'd never get into the game because we'd never want to take off our warm-up outfits. My people like tracksuits way too much. Also, if you factor in the Kardashians, who are half Armenian, my people have actually ruined more basketball careers than we've ever created.

Even if my basketball dreams died, Shaq was still my gateway drug into rap music. In third grade, I asked for Jay-Z and Master P CDs during Christmastime instead of toys. My mom bought me a seven-disc CD player that I hooked up to all the speakers in the house so I could blast music when she wasn't home. Erie didn't have a hip-hop station, so I would stay up until midnight on Mondays to record the college station's hip-hop night on cassette tape. Rap helped me find my identity. It helped me relate and make friends in the rough neighborhood where we lived. It taught me to save money so I could buy a silver chain and a charm from Millcreek Mall at Piercing Pagoda that looked like the platinum one Jay-Z wore.

Rap really was an outlet for me during a rough time as a kid. My parents got divorced when I was eight, and my dad eventually started dating an eighteen-year-old high school student. At that time, my mom was going through her second divorce, after having my brother. So when I was in sixth grade I started rebelling, drinking, smoking—not weed yet, just Black & Mild cigars my friends and I stole. My grades were terrible and got me kicked off the middle school basketball team. I started writing raps and reciting them to my friends. One day my mom found them and was shocked that I was rapping about sex and being a gangster. I assured her I was doing neither of those things but confessed that I did smoke a Black & Mild in her house one day—it wasn't my uncle. As my behavior worsened, my single mom sent me to live with my father in St. Petersburg, Florida, for a year so she could sort things out and move to a better neighborhood in Erie.

Initially, going to Florida fixed nothing for me. My dad lived in a neighborhood rougher than the one I had been living in in Erie, and I started smoking weed habitually that summer before seventh grade. One night I got dragged into going to a youth group with a friend I smoked weed with. He was doing community service at this church after being charged with arson. One of the youth pastors was Carlos— not your average pastor—a Christian rapper with a humongous 'fro who gave me his group's CD after service. I went home that night, listened to the CD, and wanted to go back to youth group the next week. I kept going back: I was going twice, three times a week. Carlos helped me accept Jesus into my life, he invited me to a rap concert at a church in Tampa called Crossover, the first hip-hop church in the United States.

In no time, I formed my own Christian rap group called C.R.I.S.I.S, which stands for "Christian Rappers Influenced by Scripture Infiltrating Satan." How does one infiltrate Satan? Abstinence raps. I would sit in my room as a teen and write the most innovative punch lines about denying sex— sex I was not being offered. I remember writing lyrics that went "I love God with my mind, I love God with my heart, your girl I don't Noah (know her), tell her get off my arc." That was me at thirteen, using the story of Noah's Ark as a metaphor to tell women to hop off my dick. Carlos and I still talk, he is now married and works as an abstinence counselor in Erie, Pennsylvania—life is funny like that.

One day, I was looking for beats on a website called SoundClick—not to be confused with the now popular site SoundCloud. Back in my days there was no cloud, just a click. I stumbled on a page for an artist named Ruslan, I looked at his bio and was like "whaaaatt?" He was also a Christian rapper and an Armenian refugee from Azerbaijan, living in San Diego. I messaged him and we began talking on the phone regularly, praying, and working on music. His story was similar to mine, his parents got divorced, he was struggling to find meaning, and the church gave him a purpose.

My best friend A.J. in college at Florida State University was from San Diego. I mentioned I knew someone from there named Ruslan. He looked puzzled, "Ruslan that raps in church?" I was like, "Yeah," and he said, "My big brother is friends with him." A.J. and I decided to go to San Diego for spring break my freshman year and Ruslan invited me to stay at his house. A.J. and I went snowboarding and hung out, but then I would go to Ruslan's. When I first met Ruslan we immediately spoke to each other in broken Russian playfully saying words like *pipiska* (*penis*). Entering his mom's house felt familiar. Every Armenian's house has similar vibes, they have house slippers for every guest, food when needed, and tea and Russian candies on tap. Ruslan's mother worked at a casino and his dad was actually kind of well off, he owned an online business selling women's shoes from Russia—not any women's shoes, but the see-through pumps worn by strippers. I made fun of Ruslan for the niche market his dad cornered—the father of a Christian rapper sells shoes for strippers, I'm not judging, Jesus was into sex workers. When I hung around Ruslan we got along, but we would argue all the time about Christianity. I was pretty radical in my faith, I thought Christians should speak in tongues, exorcise demons, and perform miracles, and I thought God was always speaking to me. Ruslan was a lot more practical.

Fifteen years later, I'm an atheist who no longer raps but is a stand-up comedian living in New York City. To this day Ruslan still raps for Jesus. He's actually very successful and well known in the industry, and it's a full-time job for him. He tours all over the country, and whenever he comes to NYC, we always hang out, and it makes for some very interesting conversations, which we started recording on his YouTube show. One of the videos is titled *Ex-Christian Rapper Turned Atheist Comedian Rufat Agayev.* The comments on the video are wild, with many Christians commenting that because I left the faith I was never truly a Christian to begin with.

> You cannot have been truly saved and leave. . . . Unless you come back. . . . And that's backed by the scriptures not my opinion

I remember one night I met up with Ruslan at a diner after a show of his in Brooklyn, he was with a group of young Christians, some of them rappers. He introduced me as his Armenian brother and told them I used to believe back in the day. One kid asked why I stopped believing. I told him I could never come to grips with a specific passage of scripture in the Bible.

Samuel 15:3

Now go, attack the Amalekites and totally destroy
all that belongs to them. Do not spare them; put to
death men and women, children and infants, cattle and
sheep, camels and donkeys.

I told the young man that I couldn't reconcile believing
in a god that commanded his people to commit genocide,
to kill women and children. In the movie *Scarface*, Scarface
vows to never kill women or children, "No wife, no kids!"
Was Scarface more moral than God? The young man started
to get combative and told me that I need God's love. He was
like those YouTube comments coming to life. He was having
a C.R.I.S.I.S.

That's when Ruslan stepped in and said, "Rufat raises some
valid points. We both fled what could've been a genocide. It's
not wrong to question scripture." It meant a lot that he stood
up for me right then. I never really grasped until that moment
how important our shared connection as refugees was. I had
so many Christian friends from my past who are amazing
people that I have fallen out of touch with. I've had mentors
and close friends who stopped talking to me after I expressed
that I was leaving the faith.

Ruslan and I couldn't just break our friendship because
I no longer believe Jesus is Lord. I can look Ruslan in the
eyes and tell him there is no god and he can tell me that I
need god, and our friendship doesn't weaken. I believe we
get a kick out of trying to offend each other because our bond
as refugees from Azerbaijan is stronger than any man-made
religion. Shared experiences are a fast track to connection,
it's why we try to relate to each other, why the military and
college fraternities perform group hazing rituals, why I am

still friends with someone on the other side of the country because, goddamn it, we fled!

RUFAT AGAYEV immigrated to the United States from Baku, Azerbaijan, as a refugee with his parents in 1992. He graduated from Florida State University and now lives in Brooklyn where he is a New York–based stand-up comedian, writer, and actor. His incisive style and dynamic approach drive the observations and stories that make up his comedy. Rufat was a finalist in New York's Funniest in 2019 at the New York Comedy Festival. You can see Rufat perform all over the country at clubs such as Carolines on Broadway and DC Improv. He's been featured on popular live comedy shows and podcasts like *Comedy at the Knitting Factory*, *Comedians You Should Know*, *The Unofficial Expert*, and *The Book of Ye*.

My China

BY AGUSTINUS WIBOWO

This piece was performed in Ubud, Indonesia, October 2018

I was raised on stories from China, the land of my ancestors. The magnificent Great Wall that resembles a giant dragon lying across the mountains and desert. The legendary monkey king who can transform himself into various animals and objects. The goddess who flies to the moon after drinking a magical potion. The fearless and patriotic warriors from the epic of the Three Kingdoms.

While reading those bedtime stories to me, Mama used to say, "Grow up quick, my dear, grow up. One day you will return to Chung Kuo, the land of your ancestors. But don't forget, take Papa and Mama along with you."

I grew up in Indonesia during Suharto's New Order regime. Back then, being a Chinese minority in this country was not easy. You were not allowed to have your own Chinese name. You were not allowed to speak your Chinese language. You were not allowed to openly practice your

Chinese rituals. You were not even allowed to say that name with pride: Chung Kuo.

In the anti-communist Indonesia, Chinese people were suspected of being communists, of being materialistic and unpatriotic to Indonesia. We might have been citizens, but we were seen as inferior ones. People on the streets used to mock me because of my slanted eyes. That's how I grew up thinking that there were only two types of people in this world: those with slanted eyes and those with rather large ones.

And thus, I cultivated the dream to return to the motherland. To the magical land of those gods and heroes. To the land where I would be protected by my ancestral brothers and sisters. To the land where I would never need to be ashamed of my eyes.

When I was nineteen, I got the opportunity to study in China. My parents sent me to a university in Beijing, so that I could learn about my roots. I dreamed of an epic homecoming; of being welcomed warmly by my fellow Chinese brothers and sisters. But in reality, I was not seen as a homecoming compatriot. It turned out, the blood of my ancestors inside me was nothing more than blood. With my Indonesian passport, I was simply a foreigner, who had to pay the same expensive tuition fees as students from Angola or America. I also couldn't understand the Chinese language I heard spoken, as I only knew a few hundred words. On the other hand, Chinese people couldn't understand my Chinese, as I spoke it with the wrong tones.

It was hard for me to accept that there were almost no smiles on people's faces on the street, unlike in Indonesia, where smiling is part of the culture. Chinese people looked very serious to me, and they talked very loudly as if quarrelling with each other. It was even harder to adjust myself to use the public toilets on a regular basis, as they were full of wet waste and buzzing flies. But the worst thing of all was the spit. When I was a kid, Mama used to teach me: "Never spit like those Indonesians! We Chinese never spit!" But I found out that the Chinese in China do spit—from the bottom of their throat, "hoooak, thuuu."

As I took in all these unusual things, I wondered whether we were indeed the same fellow Chinese. Did we really come from the same ancestors?

Nevertheless, being in China was not all that bad. There, for the first time in my life, I could walk with my back straight and my head held high. I didn't need to hide my skin color and slanted eyes anymore.

However, it slowly began to bother me. In Indonesia, to be Chinese meant to be different, to be treated differently. Even though this special treatment was unpleasant more often than not, there was something special about being different. It gave me a sense of uniqueness and exoticism, which I was sometimes proud of. It gave me a sense of self.

But in China, I just looked like all the people around me. I felt like I became faceless, anonymous. I lost myself. I felt the urgency to look different from all these people. I needed really badly to show them that I was a "foreigner." So I started to wear the Indonesian skullcap and sarong wherever I went, including to attend classes at the university. It was my way of emphasizing my Indonesian-ness.

But my Indonesian patriotism was not without sacrifices. The sarong gave me lots of troubles when I was riding my bicycle. It often slipped inside the wheel, and I would fall off the bike. On many occasions, people gathered around me, looked at me in disbelief, wondering: Who is this crazy man wearing a woman's skirt?

I lived in China for nine years, and I felt that my identity was just "being a foreigner." In Indonesia I was Chinese, and in China I was Indonesian. I ended up feeling like I belonged nowhere.

When I returned to Indonesia, I found that my father was an old man already, lying in bed, fighting against the stroke that had paralyzed half of his body. I thought it was time to show my devotion as a son. So I said to him, "Papa, get well soon. And then, I will take you to fulfill your lifelong dream: to return to your motherland."

"No, no, no," my father said. "You are wrong. That's not returning to the motherland. That's just going to China. Our motherland is here, Indonesia."

I could hardly believe what I was hearing. My father was once jailed by the Suharto regime for a year, for merely attending a protest against the government for the violation of the basic rights of the Chinese community in our town. He has suffered racial discrimination and witnessed at least two waves of bloodshed against the Chinese.

But all that bitterness had evaporated. He said, "Our motherland is here, Indonesia."

Since the fall of Suharto in 1998, Indonesia has changed dramatically. This also brought dramatic changes to the Chinese community in this country. Chinese people can now have Chinese names, speak Chinese languages, celebrate Chinese New Year, practice Chinese culture, believe in Chinese religions. They can work as civil servants or be elected as political leaders. Being Chinese no longer means being second-class citizens.

My China turned out to be different from my father's China. My China is about being a minority, about the fantasies of a flawless motherland. When I was in Indonesia, being a minority made me miss China, and when I was in China, my fantasies made me reject the real China. But my father's China was about accepting his own reality, about the reconciliation of seemingly conflicting identities. Indonesia has accepted him as Chinese, and he has accepted Indonesia as his home.

He said: "Everything starts in your mind. If you feel you're a minority, then you will be forever a minority. If you feel you're a second-class citizen, then you will forever be a second-class. If you feel you're a victim, then you will forever be a victim."

He made me realize I was a small fish searching for the ocean, but I could never find it, because I kept rejecting all the oceans around me, which I only saw as water.

––––––

AGUSTINUS WIBOWO is a travel writer. A descendant of Chinese immigrants, the question of identity dominated his earlier life and shaped his perspective. The quest for answers has taken him to many different parts of the world, including Afghanistan, where he stayed for three years as a journalist. He also loves to venture along the obscure borders and to blend into various minority groups. His work has pioneered a new genre in Indonesian travel literature by allowing readers to experience the writer's physical and emotional journey as they contemplate their own conflict and anxieties. His third book, a travel memoir, *Zero: When the Journey Takes You Home*, became a national bestseller and will soon be adapted into a film. His latest work, *Us and Them*, which reveals the roots of human identities and conflicts, will be published in 2022.

Don't Follow Your Dreams (Especially, the American Dream)

BY EMMA RAMOS

I was ten when my born-and-raised-and-never-leaving-Mexico-'cause-who-would-leave-Mexico-if-everything-is-in-Mexico Mexican parents drove nineteen hours and fifty-nine minutes to take me to Disneyland.

Now, you need to know I grew up extremely sheltered. My book collection consisted of *Enciclopedia Cumbre, Enciclopedia de las Bellas Artes,* and *Colección de Cuentos de Disney 20 Tomos.* The *Disney Storybook Collection* was my most valuable possession. It was conceived before I was conceived: my grandma bought it from a door-to-door salesman in the 1960s for her grandchildren, before she had grandchildren. I've seen every Disney film made, from the 1930s onward. Get the picture?

This trip to Disney was *the* trip. We had our road-trip music on: *Little Mermaid*'s "Part of Your World" on repeat. What a great song to have on the way from Mexico to Disneyland. *Wouldn't you think my collection* (aka life, was about to be) *complete?* (I was going to be) *part of YOUR WORLD.*

We stopped in San Diego for the night, and I went to bed dreaming my first American dream. To meet Cenicienta, Blanca Nieves, and Tribilín. That's right, you may know him as Goofy, but to me, he's forever Tribilín.

I started seeing cracks in my American dream the next morning, when I woke up to learn someone had smashed my dad's car window and stolen my Twinkies. None of Disney's twenty storybooks prepared me for some Twinkie-stealing assholes! My parents suppressed their anger so as not to ruin this "magical" trip for me, even though my "collection" was now *definitely not complete.* Especially when we got to Disneyland only to discover Tinkerbell was human-size and could *not fly.*

"Never having an American dream again!" said ten-year-old Emma. The next nineteen hours and fifty-nine minutes back home felt, *What's that word again?* (when you are trying to recover from a crushed dream, so you go back to your strict Mexican Catholic household where you still can't watch MTV or go outside in short shorts because men mistake that as a sign for permission to kidnap and rape you?) *Oh yeah* (there's no word.)

I bet my coming-of-age story was a hair different than yours. At my secundaria, ACT and GPA were just letters. No one was popping Adderalls to get into Harvard. Our grading system was 10 = great; 8 = adequate, 5 or 4 = dumb Catholic kid; lower than 4, you'd be put on Development of Thought Skills (DHP), where they made you crawl around the classroom to develop your brain cells. Our sex ed was a fifteen-minute '90s cartoon of two cats rubbing against each other, narrated by a depressed *Price Is Right*'s Rich Fields-esque voice. We did not get condoms at the end of class. AIDS was an American thing. The prerequisite for girls was to stay virgins until marriage, and then we'd fully comprehend intercourse seconds after going up the altar to a cis-man and saying, "I accept this man I barely know to enter my body and handle my life. PS, I must give him kids, or else I'm selfish. If he cheats, well, that's on me for not being able to give him kids. If I don't follow the program, I am destined to a horrible life by myself."

So, logically, instead of getting married, I became an actress. As an adult, I moved to New York, not because my mom was a drug mule, or my dad was kidnapped and beheaded. I just wanted to have an audible orgasm when I masturbated. Now *that's* my American dream.

A decade into living in the States, working as an actress, I've learned when Americans have American dreams about Mexicans, it goes something like this: a Mexican is either an illegal immigrant who crossed the border thanks to a coyote, or they flew in on a private jet packed with coke thanks to Gloria Estefan and Ricky Martin. People don't understand that most Mexicans are here thanks to Rich Barton, owner of "*el espidia*," or, Expedia. Now, if Mexicans are narrowly portrayed on TV, as an actress, it means I am narrowly eating. And I love food. Food reminds me of intermission.

Intermission! This is where I ask everyone to get a cocktail and come back to play a little game called "check-in." I learned this at my three-year acting conservatory program. (Money-greatly-spent.)

Hi, what's your name? Bill! I'm going to call you, Bill. Are you

enjoying my story? Now I've told you a bit about myself, do you feel
you understand my experience a bit more? Actually, I don't care.
For once, I AM THE PROTAGONIST, BILL. Let me break
it down for you a little more, Bill. Bill, imagine you want to be a
bullfighter. Nothing wrong with that. Completely honorable. It's just
crazy. Where are you from, Bill? New Jersey, great. So many of you
in New Jersey are trying to become hardworking "matadores" right
now, but nobody cares. That's why you want to go to Spain, because
you want to go where people do care. You tell yourself, I know Span-
ish: "Dónde está la biblioteca" will take me places. You are not afraid
of being gored to death; hey you are not even ashamed if Antonio
Banderas tells you "signor doesn't look very matadorean." You know
you have "it." Congratulations, Bill. You got your bull visa. You are
in Spain now, wearing that costume you saw once in that Madonna
video. But hey, Bill. You know what? Even though you're so good at
it, Bill. You will always say "oh-lay," not olé.

That's basically the same conversation I had. Nothing
wrong with being an actress, very honorable. At our local
theater, there were ample opportunities, if you were light-
footed. Because the theater's budget went toward buying the
biggest proscenium velvet curtain without checking if its up-
and-down mechanism adequately worked. So you could be
in the middle of being Mexican Cleopatra "No more but e'en
a woman, and commanded blah blah blah" in Spanish and
SHABAAAAM! The curtain could fall on your head. I decided I needed to go places. Grow as an artist.

No one told me I'd be fighting twenty-five bulls coming
at me, shitting on my face. And by bulls shitting on my face,
I mean paying ten times the lease as a security deposit for
not having a guarantor, Joe the Mover canceling last minute, crying to Pablo at the deli to get last-minute cardboard

boxes, renting a U-Haul, driving across town with a learner's permit and no copilot, dealing with so many rats, getting new nicknames such as the "chic peasant" (by an artistic director of an opera company), or "disabled talent" (by my first manager who said being Mexican and speaking Spanish was my "crutch"). And so on. But despite this, I don't die gored through the neck; I wake up every day to get that metro card and head to that overpriced kombucha coffee shop to get my almond latte. I remind myself: *The L is silent, and the A is not emphasized: "Aw-[really tiny L]-mond." Keep your tongue barely touching the roof of your upper palate when you get to the tiniest L.*

I started speaking English when I was six years old. With Barry White. In my house, Barry White was considered one of the best voices in the world. What was he saying? Who knows. Who cares? Other kids had Barney the dinosaur, I had Barry "the walrus of love." For hours I'd stare at those small slits between his huge eyebrows and giant cheeks, and Barry would gaze back at me on my dad's vinyl. When my dad would scream "EMMA, dónde está el control remote de la television?"—that's Spanish for "where the fuck is the remote control?"—I'd pull that remote control from between the couch cushions and reply: *I found what the world is searching for. Here, right here, my dear, I don't have to look no more.*

But being able to recite Barry White lyrics precisely as he says them does not mean you speak perfect English, and that Hollywood will embrace you immediately.

"Oh, but Emma, your English is so excellent. I *barely* hear an accent."

Well, thank you, politically correct person who is lying to my face.

I mean, I've done everything. I took Neutral American Speech classes, I watched *The Brady Bunch*, I even joined Jdate, and nothing works. Tremendous letdown because, in Mexico, I was considered the gringa 'cause I did not fake laugh watching *Seinfeld*—I actually got it.

I've learned so much living in America. I've learned Barry White is less appropriate for every day, more suitable for in bed. I've learned I can't pronounce "January" or "almond." I've learned I can't afford an apartment like Monica's in *Friends*, or any cool New York loft apartment from early millennial movies. That Twinkies are bad for you.

I've also learned I'm an immigrant. It took a while to embrace it. The thing is, if you, as an American, go to Mexico to study performing arts and decide to stay and pursue a career, you are not an "inmigrante," you are a "foráneo," a foreigner (or "gringo tonto, wtf are you thinking? You're that much into soaps?"). The word *inmigrante* typifies chronicles of pain and strife, division of social classes. I abhor divisive, not-inclusive words. But in New York, I reclaimed it. In the theater, when we're onstage, we are equal. We play different roles, but we are all actors. We immigrants are a collective force: from the cabdriver to the person sitting on a bench, waiting for a cheap matinee ticket. Every suit who walks like a bullfighter in the financial district. Every teacher, working at TaskRabbit during the evenings to make some extra income. Every person in a wheelchair in Times Square. Every commuter from New Jersey still regretting the "move for a bigger space" move. We are all connected to this powerful thread of being immigrants. My best friends, my chosen family are all immigrants. We are Batman, protecting each other, because we are not characters from *The Brady Bunch*.

I read that second-generation immigrants are the most successful. Well, shit. Not only am I the first one, I'm also the only one. And to top it off—if any Mexican mom is reading this story, brace yourself—I don't want to have kids. I never wanted to have kids. When my friends were like "A la Lulu Niño" rocking their dolls to sleep and pretending to feed them, I had mine all lined up around my Fisher-Price table plotting how to uncover the truth behind Rainbow Brite's mysterious fake smile.

So if I'm an immigrant with no offspring, it means the story starts and ends with me. My dreams end when I die. It's wholly and exclusively on me to do something memorable. I am taking the longest, most extended, and complicated way to achieve anything. I am trying to be a successful actress on my own terms, in a place where I am seen as a stranger. I now know the American dream happens outside America. Because once you are here, there's not much sleeping.

I wake up early to memorize lines to put myself on tape or head to auditions, only to realize everyone else *did* get a bit of sleep because I'm the only one with dark circles. I get notes from my manager to retape because, in the emotional scene, my nostrils covered 75 percent of the frame. I buy some "healthy" overpriced burrito at Le Pain Quotidien before heading to the theater rehearsal and when I do the math, realize I'm making $6.25 per hour. I go shoot some funny videos with friends on the weekend, thinking I'm the Mexican Issa Rae and that I'll definitely sell my show to HBO. I update my showreels, tape more auditions—Boom! I book a costar role that turns into a recurring. I'm still getting one-liners and residual checks for $57.85, but I slowly get more work. And hey, my soundproof booth for voiceover auditions is superhelpful for my orgasms, and now that you're asking, I *did* find a date on Jdate. Yes, it's pretty exhausting following your American dream. But you know what? *I'm never, ever gonna quit 'cause, quittin' just ain't my shtick.*

EMMA RAMOS is a bilingual Mexican actress, comedian, and sketch comedy artist. She won the CenturyFox/Disney Women of Color TV Pilot Incubator as well as the Warner Media 150 Award at the 2020 Sundance Film Festival. Her sketch series *B.U.T.S.* won Best Comedy at NBCUniversal Short Film Festival and was nominated twice for the Imagen Awards. Emma's TV credits include a recurring role on *New Amsterdam*, *Law & Order: SVU*, *Unforgettable*, and *Valentina*. She was a semifinalist for Sundance's "New Voices." Her theater credits include Ivo van Hove's *Scenes from a Marriage*, *Water by the Spoonful* by Quiara Alegría Hudes, Pablo Neruda's *R&J* for the Public Theater's Mobile Unit, and *Frontières Sans Frontières* ("Ramos should win a prize for this"—*Time Out*.)

Sweet Stinking Elevators

BY ZUZANNA SZADKOWSKI

Sometimes I step into an elevator in Midtown. An old one with a little dirty round window in the door. Or one with a door that swings open to another door that slides open to reveal an interior that dips a little bit when you step in. Or I step into an elevator with a call button like a worn-down pearl or a ground-down oversize tooth. I step in, and a stink hits me. And if it's just the right stink: it's Poland. It's extra-bonus-Poland if the wall is painted two-toned: a shiny, sick pale green on the bottom, and an ancient, matte eggshell on top.

I ride in that elevator, and I feel feelings, and it just gets me fucking twisted. Because I am ill for nostalgia. I love sucking it up through my nose, soaking it in through my skin via breeze, via a particular combo of temp and dry air. When it hits me in my outfit and moves my skirt against my shins, I'm done in.

Smells and general atmospheric feelings hurt me so deeply: delicious wrenching pangs. I get hit with something, and "memory" isn't the right word. It's like a past-*something*. Maybe a time, maybe some people, maybe an event is in there somewhere, but there is always a clear hit of a feeling—of a way that I once was—of a "me" from then that I wore in a certain way, that's just better than the way I wear "me" now—of a way that I once lived that is now just a faraway dream locked forever in a stink. I want whatever "it" is back so badly in those moments. I don't want to think about it too much, because its sweet sting might give way to a kind of terror: that time moves forward and that all I actually really have is this moment.

I never lived in Poland as a sentient being. Baby-me was there, but I'll never be convinced that that's actually a real person. (The very idea that I was once small and then my bones and stuff grew is too much for me. Contemplating that strains my sanity.) No, it was young, beautiful, hopeful, talented, powerful, teen- and twenties-me—that's who spent the summers in Warsaw. (Incidentally, I think I'm now old enough to call myself "previously beautiful." Now it's sentimental instead of vain. Because, in many ways, it's so very lost. It's like what old ladies do in movies, you know: while they're running their fingers down withered old yellow photos of themselves in swimsuits, laughing with their heads thrown back, just sitting on rocks—"Oh, I was so beautiful," they say.) Beautiful-me was in Warsaw in the late nineties. I was drinking with men. I was smoking LMs and riding the tram and fantasizing. All the time, fantasizing.

Recently I got into an Uber and discovered my iPhone earbuds were missing. I fell into a dead-cold panic. It was like: *Am I gonna have to look out the window? Will I be forced to* listen *to my own brain?* I guess I no longer fantasize. I just drown my tired, doubting, punishing mind in true crime—in grisly murders—and also in fun science! My poor little throbbing brain is just poured over thick with podcasts. I sit up in bed every morning and, first thing, I turn on the Audible audiobook spigot, and I begin filling up the big hole in my head. I love the TV so much that I should be embarrassed. Housewives screaming in each other's faces? Yeah, that moves and soothes me. It feels like eating lasagna.

In Warsaw, beautiful, young, magnetic me walked the sidewalks and underpasses, through courtyards and past kiosks to nothing but the sound of her shoes clicking on sidewalk. She was just feeling herself. Feeling like a sex-thing and a charismatic-thing. In Poland, I was an American traveler with a Polish soul. My light American accent made people look up and turn their heads when I ordered a "Cola light" from the lady behind the counter. I was fresh, and I was exotic. I would visit for a few weeks, but I would fantasize about staying on, you know? Just living permanently on that block in Ochota where I was born. Eating open-faced sandwiches on buttered bread. For breakfast. Drinking hot tea from a glass. And watering plants on my balcony. I imagined breakout stardom on the Polish stage. An American–Polish ingenue. I imagined that I would walk home from the theater, and I'd be swinging a little string shopping bag, and I'd be filling it along the way with berries and lettuces and little bunches of dill. I would tuck bright, paper-wrapped peonies in the fantasy crook of my fantasy arm. And I would have those long house-keys that look like *key*-keys. You know, like an illustration of a key? Like keys to a castle? Those are the kind of keys they have in Poland. They open the locks on heavy metal Polish doors.

God, I miss being a more magical person who imagined being a more magical person.

Now I'm the now-me, and it's sad. Now, fantasizing feels like loss instead of hope. Now-me just doesn't do it. Now-me just has attitude. Back then I would hang with my Polish cohort, my bestie and sister-type friend, my European hero, Paulina. She was beautiful: tall, blond, like Claudia Schiffer. The only makeup she wore was pale-pink lipstick. She had two dresses that she wore with no bra, and she was a student of archaeology. And she loved to eat fruit. Like more than she loved to eat the good stuff. Fruit! Once, when she was walking to the university in winter this really old drunk stumbled up to her, and he got in her face and started screaming "I will fucking kill you!" He grabbed either end of the scarf she had tied around her neck, and he pulled and pulled, and he pulled them both down to their knees, and he was choking her and screaming in her face "I will fucking kill you!" Just as things were starting to look really dire, a second drunk stumbled up from behind him, and he said, "Hey, Janek, stop, stop—it's not him!" So the first drunk let go of Paulina's scarf, and he really took in the whole Claudia Schiffer thing, and he said, "Ah, you're right, it's not him" and they left. So anyway, Paulina thought that that was funny and not scary. Because she's a Polish badass. "It's funny and not scary"—that is the essence of the Polish worldview. That is one thing I learned, and I still hold on to that worldview today. For example—the fact that I used to be on a successful television show and now I'm not on a successful television show anymore? That's funny and not scary. The fact that sometimes people recognize me from said television show, and they freak out like I'm somebody special, and the whole time in my head I'm screaming *Well, where's my money? I think I should at least have some fucking money!?* That's funny and not scary. The fact that I'm forty years old is funny and not scary. See?

My dad is eighty. This is the year that he is double-me. He's lived two of my lives. Thinking about it like that, maybe I can just act like I've been given a second forty. Here's how I see it: there was this beautiful, young, powerful me who lived and thrived and withered and died. And now, I begin anew. It really works for me to think about it like that. Twenties-me never, ever gave a shit about myself post-forty. The fantasies and imaginings of my past were for a person who never turned forty. I always thought, *Who cares about the life of a forty-year-old?* Well, it turns out forty-year-olds care about that. And fifty-year-olds—I think they care about their lives, too, and I would even guess that eighty-year-olds might.

My mom died when she was sixty-five, and she was never really a whole human woman to me. Rather, she was a beast born of reaction and aggression who ate my defensiveness and was nourished by my failures. Now, it occurs to me she existed before me and outside of me. It turns out she was a lovely person. Oops. Now, I actually think I can even imagine what it would be like to be behind her face. Maybe in my second-forty iteration of self, I could have related to her, I could have empathized, or sympathized, or loved her in a way that was generous and not just selfish. She's dead and therefore currently unavailable to me, but, luckily, I have my sleep to work it out. A version of her is literally stuck in my dreamscape. She's there ready to pop out at me every single night—to yell at me, insult me, frustrate me, infuriate me so much that the dream-me has sometimes been reduced to yipping and biting like an animal. It's funny, because the dream version of her is like my mom when I was ten. She's about forty years old, just like me now. It's like my imagination is restlessly, violently battling with her/me/her as me. Like it's shaking itself awake. *My mom is dead, but I'm not dead, I'm brand-new!* my imagination seems to be saying. My imagination wants to be let out. It's screaming for fantasy and renewal.

So maybe I should go to Poland. And I should just walk

around, feeling myself. Maybe that nostalgia for Warsaw that stirs me to distraction is not a nostalgia for the past but a sort of hope-thing. A forward nostalgia if you will.

So fuck it. Let's bring on that springtime breeze. Let it shake the trees with that particular sentimental noise. And let it hit me right in the skirt. You know what I should be doing? I should be out there looking for a new elevator. Looking for an elevator that stinks like tomorrow.

ZUZANNA SZADKOWSKI was born in Warsaw, Poland, and moved to Fort Wayne, Indiana, as a small child. She lives in Brooklyn, New York, and is a professional actor, best known for playing Dorota on *Gossip Girl*. She can also be seen as Nurse Pell on the Cinemax series from Steven Soderbergh *The Knick*. Other television credits include *Search Party*, *The Good Wife*, *Elementary*, *Girls*, and *The Sopranos*. Her theater credits are various and include work off-Broadway in *Uncle Romeo Vanya Juliet* (WSJ Performance of the Year 2018); *The Crucible* and *Peter Pan* with Bedlam; *queens* at LCT3; *The Comedy of Errors* as part of The Public Theater's Mobile Shakespeare Unit; and many others. Zuzanna is also a writer. She has written several plays and screenplays and was published in the *New York Times* "Modern Love" column. Zuzanna loves documentaries, home improvement shows, and her scruffy pup, Cindy. @zuzannawanda

6

Being Here

A long-term resident paints a portrait of "Jaikisan Heights," Queens; a Dominican woman walks into a conservative bed-and-breakfast where unlikely connections are made; an Americanized Puerto Rican kid recounts his re-immersion; a "cinnamon girl" from Jersey shares her reflections on home and identity; a Norwegian American reacts to the president's mention of Norway

Stories by Suketu Mehta, Laura Gómez, Rojo Perez, Maysoon Zayid, and Siri Hustvedt

(The dates of the performances are included, as the pieces reference specific political and social events.)

Jaikisan Heights

BY SUKETU MEHTA

November 2019, Joe's Pub

I came to Jackson Heights, Queens, from Bombay when I was fourteen. Or Jaikisan Heights as we South Asians call it. My parents put me in the nearest convent school, because the Christian schools in India were the good ones. I was fresh off the boat and they put me in an all-boys school, in which I was the first minority.

So, I'm sitting at this table eating my lunch by myself, because no one else will sit with me. And this boy with red hair and freckles comes up to me and says: "Lincoln should have never let them off the plantations!" and I say, "What does that have to do with me?"

I had only one friend in my first year, and I lived for the Saturdays when I would take the bus to his house in Middle Village. The next year, another minority joined me in the school. I'm walking down the halls and someone says: "Hey Mehta! There's another Hi-en-du in school!" The new kid turned out to be a Jain, but my classmates weren't cognizant of such differences. And that was the boy who remains my best friend, Ashish. We went through fire together, dealing with teachers who thought we were pagans, and students who thought we were everything their white parents were resisting in Queens in the 1970s. There was nothing micro about the aggressions we endured.

But then, in my junior year, for no particular reason, a bunch of other misfits joined the school, and we had an entire lunch table of the excluded. So there was me and the other Hi-en-du (who was actually a Jain), there was Gilberto the Cuban (who claimed that his father was one of the Watergate burglars), there was a very short Irish angel dust addict named Quinn (other kids called him a midget, we called him the Mighty Quinn), there was the school's only out gay boy who was having an affair with the math teacher, and an Indonesian who was obsessed with cars. Everybody wanted to beat us up. But at the Lunch Table of the Excluded, we also had Han Soo Kang, the "mysterious Oriental." He was a Korean student whose mother would pack him noodles every day for lunch. He would eat his noodles in silence, just looking this way and that and not saying anything. And since he wasn't saying anything, we'd say things about him. "Kang, man, he's into that martial arts shit!"

"You hear about the black belt? Well, he's got a belt that's so secret he can't even tell you its color!" So everyone stayed clear of us because they didn't want to fuck with Kang. (He was actually the sweetest guy, who wouldn't have hurt a fly, and he ended up going to engineering school at Columbia.)

At the time I got there in the late seventies, Jackson Heights was surrounded by some pretty all-white enclaves, including East Elmhurst. But the building that we lived in was incredibly diverse. We had Indians, Pakistanis, Bangladeshis, Haitians, Dominicans, Jews, and Muslims. The building was owned by a Turkish man, but the superintendent was Greek. These were all people who had been killing each other just before they got on the plane to come to America. And here we were in Jackson Heights, in the same building, eating each other's strange foods, and dating each other's strange children. The only thing we had in common was that on Sunday mornings on a Spanish TV station, there was a TV program called *Vision of Asia* that broadcast Bollywood songs, and the entire building—Indians, Pakistanis, Bangladeshis, Haitians, Dominicans, Jews, Muslims, Greeks—sang along. It was the one thing that unified us.

In my new book, *This Land Is Our Land*, I've written about Jaikisan Heights, as a symbol of how all these people who had been killing each other banded together, not only in my building, but, as I discovered, in street gangs. I was at a party a few years ago and this Indian Gujarati cigarette bootlegger came up to me and said, "You're a professor. Please speak to my son, he's sixteen and he's going the wrong way."

He introduced me to this Indian teenager with spiky hair.

And the father said, "He's joined a street gang."

"What street gang?" I asked the kid.

And he said, "Look at this," and he showed me the initials tattooed on his neck. It said PBN, which, he told me, stands for "Punjabi Boys Network." The PBN has got Indians, Pakistanis, Bangladeshis, Afghans all from Jackson Heights, all in a gang fighting everyone else—the Latinos, the Blacks, the whites.

So I said, "Your parents are fighting each other back home,

but it's good that you're fighting together over here. What kind of gang stuff do you do?"

And he said, "Well, we go to the Kebab King and when people are leaning over the counter, looking at chicken, we pickpocket them! We get five bucks, ten bucks."

"Well, that doesn't sound that dangerous . . . Do you ever have, like, gang rumbles?"

And he said, "Yes, yes, yes. We've got a connection to the Bloods. They've got this sign," and he showed me the Bloods sign.

And I asked, "Do you have a sign? The Punjabi Boys Network?"

And he looked this way and that and he said, "I'm gonna show you the sign, but please don't show it to anyone else."

Since I love you all, and you might be in Jackson Heights someday, I'll show you the sign that will get you saved. It's an authentic sign that the gang uses. It's this.

[Bows with hands in prayer, then bows again with hands in gun symbol].

I said, "That's an interesting sign, what does it mean?"

And he said, "It means 'Namaste, motherfucker'!"

So now, I use it with my South Asian friends. "Namaste, motherfucker"—"I bow to thee, motherfucker."

Queens is, of course, famous not just for this gorgeous mosaic. The most diverse neighborhood in the country is also the birthplace of the least diverse man in the country. Donald Trump was born in a place called Jamaica Estates, which was an all-white enclave when he was growing up. When I recently went to Jamaica Estates, it was filled with Bangladeshis and Jamaicans and all kinds of people—we overwhelmed them through sheer fecundity, as we will do in the country as a whole. What we're seeing now in the country is a battle of two Queens. The Queens of today hasn't seen any major ethnic conflict since the 1990s. New York is the safest big city in the nation, although it is far from being the most egalitarian. Two out of three New Yorkers are immigrants or their children. And it is this which was deeply threatening to this man from Jamaica Estates, Queens, which represented exclusivity and exclusion. I wrote the book because of the language that Donald Trump was using about immigrants when he was president. He referred to immigrants as robbers, rapists, criminals, and drug dealers. He was often going on about our family values. And, mostly, when speaking about these family values, he was speaking about Mexican immigrants.

So I decided to see what it is exactly that he was afraid of.

I went down to a place called Friendship Park on the US–Mexico border. If you go just south of San Diego, there's a wall, which stops just before it comes to the sea. Right before it gets to the Pacific Ocean, there's a small stretch of land that was inaugurated under the Nixon administration in 1971. It's called Friendship Park, and it was meant for people in the US who couldn't leave and come back in. If you don't have papers and you're on the US side of the border, you can approach the border without being asked for your papers. In the seventies, you could sit down with your family, because there was no wall or fence, just a boundary marker. They would come from the Mexican side, and you could have a picnic with them, you could give them a hug, and then they would go back to Mexico and you'd come back here to the US. Through successive administrations, that patch of land became less open. Under the Obama administration bollards were added, so you could still go there and hang out with your family, but you couldn't actually sit down and have a picnic. Under the Trump administration an ugly industrial mesh fence was put up.

I went down there for two weeks, and I learned about family values. You're only allowed to go there for ten minutes at a time, on weekends. I saw a Mexican man who hadn't seen his mother for seventeen years. He was undocumented and he'd come to the US so he could send his mother money. For seventeen years he'd been sending her money every single week. And finally, he'd come all the way from Colorado, taking buses to Friendship Park, and she'd come from a distant province in Mexico. He goes up to the fence, and his mom comes up from the other side. He puts his face up to the fence, and she puts her face up. And he says, "I miss you, Mama."

And she says, "I love you."

She hasn't seen him for seventeen years. She says, "Are you eating right? You look thin."

He can't give her a hug, even though all he wants to do is give her a hug. He told me later that he could feel his mom's breath on his face—he could smell her. He put his hand up to the fence, and he put his pinkie finger through. And she put her pinkie finger through. Because that's the only contact that the gap in the fence will allow. And they do this thing which the immigrants call the "pinkie kiss"—the pinkies touching each other. All along the fence, mothers and children, husbands and wives, best friends doing this kissing of the pinkies. It's the most emotional reporting I've ever done.

After my first day at Friendship Park, I ran to my car and I called up my parents in New Jersey and told them how much I missed them. If you've ever felt distanced from someone in your family, go to this place and see what happens when bureaucrats and politicians keep you from your mother. Keep you from giving a hug to your family.

For immigrants, it's not about "chain migration" as the Republicans like to call it. The family for us isn't a chain, it's a safety net.

———————

SUKETU MEHTA is the author of *This Land Is Our Land: An Immigrant's Manifesto* and *Maximum City: Bombay Lost and Found*. He is a professor of journalism at New York University.

The Great Divide:
On a Trip Upstate,
Learning to Listen

BY LAURA GÓMEZ

May 2019, Joe's Pub

It was late July and we were weeks away from shooting the final season of *Orange Is the New Black*. I had been informed by our producers that we would continue exploring the journey of my character, Blanca Flores, who on Season 6 had been caught by the Immigration and Customs Enforcement Agency, commonly known as ICE.

Immersing myself in my role meant getting in touch with organizations that deal with issues of families being separated and the mistreatment of migrants and reading a lot about current events. ICE, for instance, was created in 2003 under the Bush administration, using the terrorist attacks of 9/11 as an excuse to "protect" the United States from the "threat" of illegal immigration. Later on, President Obama was often criticized for his massive deportations of illegal immigrants. Meanwhile, Donald Trump tends to define immigrants as savages and to curse Hispanics with the label of criminals and "bad hombres" as a way to maintain the myth that undocumented Latinos are here to take what righteously belongs to white people, with the occasional "I suppose there are exceptions" utterances of his.

Before filming began, I desperately needed a break. I had decided to take one last summer trip and was on my way to visit my cousin's in-laws in a little town upstate. This lovely couple lives in a beautiful house surrounded by nature, so warm and cozy that it feels like a sanctuary.

The seven-hour commute by train started with a majestic view of the Hudson River—a magical journey in comparison to the hectic few months I had been living—inviting me to enjoy a peaceful time and relax. My hosts had prior commitments, so we had agreed that they would pick me up at the station a bit later than my estimated time of arrival, which gave me some time to kill.

By the time I got there, I was quite hungry, and a person working at the station told me about a bed-and-breakfast across the tracks. Right away I saw a big American flag waving tall and proud, making me feel a bit anxious, as I'm wary of the nationalistic subtext these patriotic symbols sometimes carry.

I went in, and a middle-aged white woman, the Boss Lady, cautiously greeted me. I asked if the kitchen was open, she replied that it was a bit early, but noticing my disappointment said not to worry, her brother was already there and he could prepare something for me to eat.

The next room was set up like a small restaurant, with a massive flat-screen TV featuring Fox News in all its glory.

I sat by the bar. Seated next to me was a younger version of Boss Lady, her sister, concentrating on the television, as the news anchor informed the world that a *beautiful, blond, white* woman had been raped and killed by an *illegal Mexican immigrant* and her body had been found by a runner near a trail, the whereabouts of the killer still unknown. This information was repeated over and over again emphasizing the physical description of the victim, and the ethnicity and legal status of the perpetrator.

The action was horrific and certainly deserved punishment, but Fox News clearly wanted its audience to keep certain fears in mind. The language the anchor used not only perpetuated stereotypes, but it seemed to have been designed to associate the crime to a whole ethnic group, instead of condemning the individual who actually committed it. Not only do such stereotypes spread misinformation, they create unfounded biases toward diversity and "otherness."

So here I was, with my big curly hair and slight accent, visibly different from those around me, and in a way more similar—at least physically—to the individuals criminally profiled on these type of news cycles. Even though I'm a US citizen, a mere technicality given the circumstances, it was a rather uncomfortable scenario.

I managed to place my order: a salad, a soup, and a seltzer water. I kept my calm in spite of the consistent strategic message being delivered via the screen—that anyone foreign is some sort of enemy.

A minute or two later, the Boss Lady came back with a tall glass of seltzer water. I thanked her but told her I did not need the straw she was about to give me. I have been adamant about not using them for their negative impact on the planet, and even though I did not express this, she seemed annoyed and offended. A bit over-the-top, I thought, but then realized that Fox News had probably told her that the non-straw-water-drinker-extremists want to get rid of her old American values.

"Some people need them, you know," she said in high-pitched voice. In a respectful manner I replied that of course, if anybody needs a straw, they should have the right to use it. I could immediately detect an invisible boundary and a certain distance in her body posture.

The tension was broken by two beautiful little boys who came out from the kitchen. The children ran to greet her, calling her Grandma, her large body bending over to kiss their pink cheeks. Their parents walked behind them, and they all had a brief chat about some family barbecue. The couple eventually nodded, acknowledging my presence. I said hello, with the biased news of the Mexican immigrant running nonstop in front of our noses, making me wonder, Is that what they think we are? Barbaric criminals waiting for them to turn their back in order to attack them? I didn't ask.

After they left, the Boss Lady told me she had three sons, one of them a landscape gardener, while the other two worked for Homeland Security, proudly adding that her youngest works for ICE. I have no idea why she mentioned it, maybe because she could see my Hispanic heritage, and if I was "illegal" this could serve as a warning. Or maybe it was just where our casual conversation took her. No matter the reason, I felt my blood rushing through my veins, especially having experienced intense emotions around this issue after interpreting a character on television who was placed in a detention center in a tear-jerking finale that left everyone so deeply affected, I still get messages about it. Blanca Flores is a fictional character, but her destiny reflected a little bit of the cruel reality we're currently living in.

For a second there, I felt I was part of some absurd parody, the protagonist of a ridiculous sitcom or a Jordan Peele horror movie, in which a Latina comes into the house of a small-town white family asking for shelter only to find herself persecuted under the suspicious eyes of the family members, all brainwashed by Fox News. Or perhaps it was the universe with its peculiar sense of humor wanting me to do some active research by actually feeling discriminated against based solely on my looks. In essence, the planned misinformation on the TV, and the ignorance I was witnessing wasn't fiction, it was real life being presented before my eyes.

As the Boss Lady's brother came out with my soup and large salad, my curiosity got the best of me. I wanted to know more about this woman and her son, the ICE agent, so I put on the imaginary seat belt and asked some further questions. She mentioned that he had an annoying girlfriend who "just likes to read and travel."

"A liberal?" I asked with an obvious smirk on my face.

"Yes, yes she is," she responded with disdain, adding that her son obviously wants to save her, but it's not his place to do so.

I tried hard not to laugh at her comment. I thought maybe it was the other way around, and this young woman was the one thinking this guy could change. In any case, I did my best to keep it together and simply told her I had a feeling life would take care of it. She seemed relieved to think these two wouldn't last.

Her sister finally tore herself away from the news and timidly intervened, asking where I was from.

"I'm from Dominican Republic," I said, not sure if they knew this was a different country from Mexico—my own prejudices, one might say—"but I've been living in the city for nineteen years, so I'm a bit of a New Yorker."

Her eyes widened as she explained with a big smile how much she loves New York. The sisters once spent seven hours there and she found it fascinating. The Boss Lady, on the other hand, thought the city was too noisy. They asked what I was doing all the way up in their town. I had the unique pleasure of answering "just traveling," feeling quite amused with my response. Then I told them that I like going upstate to connect with nature, and that it reminds me of my country, in the sense that people know each other and there's a sense of community. The sister seemed satisfied, while the matriarch looked at me with a quizzical gesture, not knowing what to make of my presence there, of what I was saying, or the fact that I was way different from the image of an immigrant she had pictured in her head.

The conversation somehow took us to the subject of student loans. I mentioned how unfair it was that the US government abused its citizens in this regard, and in a frustrated tone she explained how her sons were probably "gonna be paying off their debts till the end of their days."

I could have said how much closer she was in many ways to most immigrants she's been told to despise and blame for her misfortunes. I wanted to ask her about the elections and say, *I'm a liberal, who reads and travels, just like your potential daughter-in-law.* I could have asked *Why do you like Trump? Do you know he's a racist, narcissist, and misogynist and that there are other outlets for information aside from Fox News? Do you know that most immigrants are decent, hardworking people and that these*

assholes on your TV are brainwashing you? Are you really a Christian? 'Cause Christ would have never approved of bigotry and the separation of families.

And finally, I wanted to ask: *How can you and your son sleep at night?*

Instead, I simply asked for the check. She gave it to me and I pointed out there must have been a mistake. She was charging me $5, and the salad alone was $16. She politely answered that she liked me and was only charging me for the small soup. While her response caught me by surprise, I accepted the gesture, paid the bill, and said my goodbyes.

This whole lunch hour felt quite surreal. Although it forced me to listen, I hate that I couldn't do more to make her understand that in reality, the government she supports has done nothing more than to bring out the cancer that for years has been dormant underneath society's skin, giving a platform to a racism and sexism that deeply and negatively affects us all. I assumed she, like many others, admired Donald Trump because she believed he was keeping Americans safe, when in fact, by placing us all against one another, through race, identity, and religion, he was making sure the old technique of "divide and conquer" worked as designed. I've even heard some documented Latinos in the US hide behind their privilege and defend him by saying that when he demonizes immigrants he's talking about the "bad ones," not them. Thus, here we are, living through extremely hostile and alienating times, barely capable of dialogue, more disconnected than ever before.

It was a confusing experience for us both. It would have been so much easier for me if "they," the Fox News watchers, really were the obscene caricature "we liberals" would like them to be, and easier for her if I had been the vulgar immigrant she's been told that I am. But neither of us was that, and as much as I could recognize her limitations, I knew she was not a monster—just a protective mother, a loving grandma, and a product of her environment. There's nothing I could have said or done to change her mind on politics. All I could do was to be a decent human being who defied whatever stereotypes she has been fed. All I could do was leave her thinking, *Well, that Dominican lady was actually pretty nice.*

———

LAURA GÓMEZ is a Dominican actress, writer, and director. Gómez is best known for her portrayal of the character Blanca Flores in the Netflix series *Orange Is the New Black*. She divides her time between New York and Santo Domingo.

The River

BY ROJO PEREZ

March 2018, Joe's Pub

In 1994 my parents finished their "American dream." After twenty-plus years of snowstorms, long hours of minimum wage, robberies, countless lottery tickets, and learning how to say specifically without an *e* at the beginning, they were ready to go back home. "Especifically" was a big hurdle to clear.

My dad was a truck driver with an eighth-grade education, who was forced to leave school and work in the sugarcane fields in San Sebastian, Puerto Rico, to provide for his mom and five siblings. Having heard about the opportunities in "America" from those who had left, and tired of working all day under the sun, at eighteen he left the only place he had known and landed in New York—aka Puerto Rico of the North. My mom, who got her associate at EDP College in San Sebastian, found herself working for the city as a secretary at the Labor Department after having worked the line in multiple factories.

A lot of people come to the States from their poorer countries for a better life. My parents came in on some *Inside Man* shit. They came in, treated it like a heist, played the system for multiple decades, and left before greed took them over.

They finally saved up enough to build a home back in Puerto Rico and live that slower-paced life near family and friends they always wanted. Only issue was, they had this eight-year-old chubby Americanized boy who hated being outside, knew no Spanish, and connected more with *Saved by the Bell* than *El Chavo*. More New Kids on the Block than Tito Puente, McDonald's fish filet over rice and beans–type kid. I was the original Manny from *Modern Family*. In an effort to provide a better life for me, my parents were raising a gringo with a killer tan.

At eight years old, I woke up one day and all my stuff was packed. I remember this was not discussed—no family meeting, no votes were tallied. Good lesson to learn about life: people with power can make unilateral decisions. A bit heavy for an eight-year-old to process, but still, good lesson. All I was told was I'd never have to wear a winter coat again and San Sebastian had plenty of space for me to be outside. What they happened to leave out, and what I found out when we got there, was that Puerto Rico is consistently 90 degrees, and mosquitoes were not shy about showing me their affection. I'd sit in the back of my new classroom, with kids who looked like me but I had nothing in common with, just thinking about why everything was so dusty. I was a real delicate kid.

I remember my dad once asked me to help him work on the car and I walked out with yellow dishwashing gloves because I knew how hard it was to get grease out from under your fingernails. I was not about that dirty hand life. Hence why I'm up here now.

So back to school; I had a lot of free time—turns out it's pretty easy to zone out when you don't really know the language. Those early days my favorite class was lunch, the only hour in the day I didn't feel lost. Turns out "French fries" is universal.

My parents feared I would become a third-grade dropout whose only marketable skill was quoting Steve Urkel and doing the Ravishing Rick Rude dance. After school, and sometimes before school, I'd run out in the living room with a blanket cape around my neck in my turtle underwear and do the "I'm too sexy" dance. Realizing that dancing as a seminaked eight-year-old probably wasn't a smart career beginning for me, they found an English-speaking private school an hour away and paid for it with long work hours and negative amounts of family vacation. All they did was sacrifice, come home late, tired, but I never once remember hearing them bitch about it. At least not to my face.

A few years passed, school got easier, the English definitely helped. I eventually learned enough Spanish to not sound like a total poser, I played sports, made friends. Turns out, nobody cares you can't roll your *R*'s if you can hit the baseball; it just becomes a cute quirk. My parents worked and worked and worked, they seemed happy and I felt happy for them, yet I still never really felt like I identified with other Puerto Ricans. In a weird way I kind of grew up with shame, feeling I was better than, not learning how to truly embrace where I came from. Embarrassed how loud people would say Puerto Ricans were.

It was pretty country where I grew up. People had horses as transportation, and at least once a week there'd be a traffic jam because someone's cows would get loose and everyone would have to wait till they decided to cross the street.

I'd show up late to school and just say, "*the cows*" like a tiny Kramer who can't catch a break, and the teacher would be like, "Yeah, that checks out. I was late, too, my kid couldn't find his pet rooster this morning."

For fun, my friends would walk through farms for miles just to go down a hidden hill where there was a river to spend some time in. People would yell at us to get off their property, we'd run from their farm animals, step in cake-size cow shits. Slapping your whole body trying to avoid getting bit up, sharing one bottle of water. And I'd be like: "For what? To spend thirty minutes, maybe an hour in some freezing water, just to turn around and walk back because it was going to get dark?" I would always wonder, "Why do we do this? Seems pointless, so much work for such a small amount of pleasure." But nobody else seemed to mind. The whole walk, my friends would talk about how great that water was gonna be. Who would be the first to swing from the rope and dive in. How they couldn't wait to hide under the waterfall, play underwater tag. And the whole walk back, they'd talk about how fun it was, who did the best trick, and when was the next time we were going.

I was eleven on September 21, 1998, when Hurricane George made landfall, a Category 3 by the time it hit that night. The power was out, the house was quiet; with a flashlight I looked at the rain and the wind. In a weird way I could actually see the wind, and I remember hearing branches break, electrical poles fall, tin roofs fly off people's homes. My parents kept pulling me inside and we tried to play cards.

None of us could focus. I was wondering what was happening outside and my parents seemed to be somewhere else mentally. See, my dad had just bought a little wood-rental business. In Puerto Rico people would rent wood to build the frames of houses and then return the wood when the cement frame was set. I swear it's true, not the most traditional business, but my dad was never a traditional guy. It was the first time he wasn't working for someone else, and remembering how proud he talked about the little business, I know he really wanted it to work. I'm sure part of it was financial, but mostly it was to prove something to himself. The only thing was, the actual business structure itself was made out of wood. When your little wood shop is in danger of disappearing because of a natural disaster, Grandma cheating at blackjack doesn't really register as a top priority.

The next morning it was drizzling, streets were a mess, still no power, no phones, no real way to communicate. We all got in the car and, at five miles an hour, drove to see what my dad's new business looked like. Passing by where houses used to be, the drive was just me looking around in shock while trying to pick up an AM radio station to see if there was any news. As we got close to where my dad's wood spot was, the ride got quiet. On the straightaway we could see the wooden building was no more. All of it was on the ground. My dad got out of the car and kind of just stared. My mom had to walk away to not cry in front of us. My dad's eyes watered, but he didn't break. A neighbor walked over and told us how and when it all came crashing down. My dad just stared straight ahead and nodded. After what felt like twenty minutes of silence, I heard my dad go: "It'll be okay, at least we don't have to rent the wood to make a new cement building." In between tears, my mom laughed and we got back in the car.

For months we worked on rebuilding what we had lost. At no point was quitting an option. This is just my experience, but it's not a unique one. All over the island there were people doing the same thing. At eleven I realized where I came from, and what it truly meant. The spirit of an island that refused to give up, that still refuses to give up. People just put their heads down and made it happen, looked ahead knowing what once was could soon be again.

After the recent Category 5 Hurricane Maria, I felt that same frustration of those long walks to and from the river. The frustration came from being seen as a second-class citizen; it reminded me of doing so much work for a fleeting moment of joy, and then having to walk back to do more work. Hearing people call us lazy, saying we are asking for handouts felt like those mosquito bites my friends and I kept slapping at. Watching the staged Puerto Rico relief efforts—seeing my people pose while 45 tossed paper towels, those are the familiar voices telling us to get off their lawn. Hearing how aid is being cut from those who truly need it—who six months after the hurricane still struggled with being displaced and had no electricity—feels like those cake-size shits we'd step in. But I remembered my friends talking about the river, how they saw what once was and what soon will be again.

Yes, it's work, but we know how great that first splash was and we know it's never gone, just waiting for us to return.

ROJO PEREZ is a New York–based comedian. Originally from Puerto Rico, Rojo moved to Florida for college and began performing stand-up comedy in local clubs and small cafés. Rojo's HBO special is titled *Entre Nos: Spot On*. In 2017 he made his late-night stand-up debut on *Conan*. Since moving to New York City he has been a cast member on MTV's *Decoded*, he was featured on Comedy Central's *Funny 'Cause It's True*, *Time Out New York*, TruTV's *Comedy Knockout*, and Univision's *Flama*. He has performed at top-tier comedy clubs across the country. In 2016 he was selected as a StandUp NBC finalist and has been a part of the Just for Laughs Comedy Festival, Moontower Comedy Festival, New York Comedy Festival, Riot LA Comedy Festival, and Akumal Comedy Festival in Mexico. Rojo's plans include one day earning enough money so that relatives will ask to borrow some, and continuing to spread laughter regardless of race, religion, or gender.

Go Back to Your Country

BY MAYSOON ZAYID

November 2018, Joe's Pub

My name is Maysoon Zayid. I was born and raised in the great state of New Jersey. Yet, my fellow Americans have been known to yell in my face, "Go back to your country!" While it's true that my home state has a bad reputation, it is most definitely part of the USA. My country is the same one those bullying me pledge allegiance to. Haters assume it is not my country for one simple reason—I am a cinnamon girl. When bigots see brown, they surmise that I am an illegal alien. Not like E.T., but like the kids caged on the Land of the Free's southern border.

I am the daughter of Ribhia Ali and Musa Zaid. My dad looks like Saddam Hussein, my mom looks like Julia Roberts, and both of them were born in Palestine. My mother came into this world an American citizen. Her father had immigrated to Utah in 1936. He was a peddler and arrived on our shores in a cargo ship. In 1959, my dad flew from Palestine to Colombia and smuggled himself to New York City. He was in the States illegally and needed a green card. So, he married the meanest woman he ever met. She knew he wasn't in it for love and they got a divorce the second he got his papers. In 1966, my dad, now an American citizen, bought a little house and flew back home to marry my mother. She was the girl of his dreams and also his first cousin. My mom has lived in that same house since the day that she landed at JFK airport many moons ago.

When I was born, my parents, who already had three little girls, didn't think that God would bless them with another one. They had only picked out a name for a boy. It was very original, you've probably never heard it—they were going to name me Mohammed. When they realized God had ignored their prayers for a son, they decided to name me Mohammadia, the chick version of the name Mohammed. Mohammed is a great name—it's the name of a prophet, and it's the name of the greatest boxer who ever lived. But being named Mohammadia is like being named Smurfette. Thankfully, doctors told my parents I was going to drop dead, and they didn't want to waste such a great name on an angel baby. Instead, they named me *Maysoon*, which is the Arabic word for *lemur*. My parents named their brown, spazzing, fuzzy baby *monkey* and I LIVED.

My mother was twenty-six years old with four children under the age of eight, when she went back to college and got a master's degree in blood banking. She went on to become chief of lab of the largest medical center in NJ. How is that for an American dream? My immigrant pops had an American dream of his own. His goal was to teach me how to walk. The doctor who delivered me was drunk, as a result, I have cerebral palsy. CP manifests itself differently in each person lucky enough to have it. Some of us are wheelchair users, some of us are nonverbal. In my case, I shake all the time, much like my comedy idol, Richard Pryor, did toward the end of his life.

The doctors told my parents that I'd never walk. Now, let me be clear, there is no shame in not walking or using any mobility device you feel frees you. My botched birth occurred before the Americans with Disabilities Act was signed. I did not have the luxury of accommodations that, unfortunately, so many people still fight for today. My father was determined to teach me how to walk because he knew it was absolutely necessary if I wanted to go to the same public school my older sisters already attended. My father would place my feet on his feet and just walk. I walked miles on that man's shoes.

When the time came, my dad marched me into Superintendent Cologreco's office to enroll me in kindergarten. Mr. C informed my immigrant father that I would not be allowed to go to school with my siblings. Instead, he recommended that I be sent to the school for children with Down syndrome. I will never forget my father, who knew nothing about the law, leaping to his feet and shrieking in his heavy Palestinian accent, "Mister Calogrecky, in the name of Allah, if you send my daughter on the short bus, I'm gonna suit you!" I'm assuming Mr. Cologreco thought my dad said he was going to shoot him instead of sue him. Either way, he complied, because when an angry Arab man waltzes into your office with his disabled daughter on his toes, and he invokes the name of Allah, you listen.

Growing up in an immigrant family in a New York City suburb is even more challenging when you're the only

Muslims in an Italian Catholic village. My parents had succeeded in mainstreaming me into the public school system. With that privilege came the burden of having to lie about Santa's existence. Santa skips Muslim chimneys because he doesn't exist. Five-year-old me knew he was a myth. Tina, my best friend since the first day of school, believed in him wholeheartedly until her sweet sixteen. My parents taught me to lie so I wouldn't break my friend's heart. Halloween was also a hassle. Halloween costumes are—not to slutshame—slutty. I say this because the costume titles literally use the word *slut*. There's "Slutty Nurse," "Slutty Mouse," and "Slutty Hillary Clinton." My conservative immigrant parents weren't fans of these risqué costumes. I had to wear a turtleneck and leggings under my red fringe flapper dress. It wasn't all that bad. New Jersey tends to be chilly on pumpkin day. I was warm and toasty while all my friends froze their slutty asses off.

Once the school year was done, my sisters and I would hop on a flight to Palestine. My parents insisted on sending me back to the motherland every single year. They were convinced that if we didn't go back, we would grow up to be Britney Spears. She's a multimillionaire. My friends would head to the Jersey Shore, and I would go to war. Tina would come and help me pack. I remember her asking me, "Are you scared? Are you scared to go to Pakistan?" and I'd be like, "Yeah, I'm terrified, which is why I'm going to Palestine." I'm no longer afraid of Karachi and I never feared the Holy Land, but I'm terrified of going to an American airport. Why? Because when I limp in, security sees an Arab. Those of you who have seen me may be thinking "How do they know you're an Arab? You could EASILY be the lost Kardashian." I'll tell you how they know—I have the kind of facial hair that no waxing in the world can deal with. Bonus—as I mentioned, I also shake all the time. So when security spies me, they're thinking, *That Arab looks nervous.* It was even worse when my dad would drop me off. He looks like Saddam Hussein and does not know how to say bye without invoking the name of Allah loudly. His fond farewells got me a one-way ticket to the glass penalty box, where passengers are randomly selected for additional screening. I am always random.

Being born to immigrant parents means that your path in life is chosen for you. We are only allowed three career choices: doctor, lawyer, or engineer. (I have no idea how engineer made the cut. I would have gone with accountant. You can make a lot of money if you learn how to play with numbers.) I was on the path to becoming an Esquire when my comedy career took off. I now play a lawyer on TV. If I didn't, I think my mother would still be disappointed in me.

After our folks have chosen our careers, they move on to matchmaking. When you're a first-generation American of Middle Eastern heritage, your parents rarely care about love. My marriage was arranged. By me. On my thirty-third birthday, I decided to get hitched, not because I was afraid of dying alone and being eaten by my cat, but because I had been a bridesmaid seventeen times. I spent $28,000 on my friends' weddings and I wanted to make my money back. To be clear, I was not desperate. If I could have married white, I would have married a guy named Mike. But my dad said he would throw himself off the George Washington Bridge if I didn't marry a Palestinian, so that simply wasn't an option. I had watched too many episodes of *Law & Order* and couldn't bear the image of the Coast Guard fishing him out all bloated and stuff.

Children of immigrants can't handle guilt. We'd rather be miserable than disappoint our parents. It takes at least one generation to develop immunity. So I went to Gaza to catch a husband. Why Gaza? They've got no place to run. It's like shooting fish in a barrel. I framed my American passport in a big gold frame and hung it around my neck like Flavor Flav. I limped through the refugee camp, waving, winking, and asking "You wanna visa, baby?" My future husband said, "Yeah!" So I said, "Pack up your stuff and let's go." He responded, "I have no stuff."

I got engaged to a starving refugee who had spent six years in political prison and brought my 90 Day Fiancé to America. When we went to apply for his green card and later his US citizenship, we were the only couple that had less than a thirty-year age gap between us. That did nothing to alleviate the struggle of naturalizing a Muslim refugee into America post-9/11. The key to our now defunct marriage was that I knew how to deal with conflict. Every time we argued, I would look at him lovingly and say: "Do you want to go back? All it takes is one call and it's Ice, Ice baby!"

I was born in the USA and I currently live in a country where Donald Trump sits in the Oval Office and leads a hateful frenzy of his supporters to chant the same taunt I have been hearing from bigots all my life: "Send Her Back!" *Her* refers to three congresswomen of color, one who is a Palestinian from Michigan and a cinnamon girl just like me. Our parents were immigrants. They are now American, and so are we. I have no problem going back to my country. I love Jersey.

MAYSOON ZAYID is an actress, comedian, writer, and disability advocate. She is a graduate of and a guest comedian in residence at Arizona State University. Maysoon is the cofounder/coexecutive producer of the New York Arab American Comedy Festival and the Muslim Funny Fest. She was a full-time on-air contributor to *Countdown with Keith Olbermann* and a columnist for the *Daily Beast*. She has most recently appeared on Oprah Winfrey Networks *In Deep Shift, 60 Minutes*, and ABC News. Maysoon had the most viewed TED Talk of 2014 and was named one of 100 Women of 2015 by BBC. As a professional comedian, Maysoon has performed in top New York clubs and has toured extensively at home and abroad. She was a headliner on the Arabs Gone Wild Comedy Tour and The Muslims Are Coming tour. Maysoon appeared alongside Adam Sandler in *You Don't Mess with the Zohan* and has written for *VICE*. She limped in New York Fashion Week, is a recurring character on *General Hospital*, and is the author of Audible's *Find Another Dream*. www.Maysoon.com

The Foreign Girl

BY SIRI HUSTVEDT

June 2018, Joe's Pub

I do not blame anyone in this audience if she or he does not remember that the malignant narcissist who currently occupies the White House once mentioned Norway. Norwegians and those of us who count ourselves as Norwegian Americans noticed. Norway popped up right after "shithole countries." The vulgarian-in-chief wondered why the US didn't attract more immigrants from "countries like Norway." Although I doubt that the man could locate the country where my mother, my paternal great-grandparents, my two uncles and aunt, ten first cousins, and myriad other cousins once or twice removed were born on the map, I suspect the Nordic country leapt into his atrophied memory banks because he had met the prime minister of Norway the day before and the word, *Norway*, even to those wholly ignorant of its people and culture, summons whiteness, blondness, and possibly skiing.

There are more US citizens becoming Norwegians these days than the other way around. Norwegians live longer than people in the rest of the world, are the beneficiaries of free universal health care and education, have maternal and paternal paid leave, the greatest gender parity in the world, the highest average incomes, and generous social programs. Why would any Norwegian decide to leave home for a country that is swiftly depriving its citizens of the few protections they do have, has adopted brutal immigration, ecological, education, and foreign policies and is led by a racist, misogynistic, xenophobic, germophobic lunatic?

My ninety-five-year-old Norwegian mother was seventeen when the Germans invaded Norway on April 9, 1940. She spent five long years under Nazi occupation. She does not need to be reminded of the fantasies of racial purity that animated National Socialism. She does not need to be reminded of the morning she woke up to the news that the Jewish family that owned the department store in her small town had been arrested in the dead of night. They were all murdered in the camps. There were Norwegian Nazis, most famously, Quisling, whose name still means "traitor" in English, but most Norwegians were ferociously opposed to the occupiers and the underground resistance was strong.

It included my mother's two older brothers, one of whom escaped to Sweden after the cell he had joined was broken. How did he get there? Sometimes stereotypes contain a piece of the truth. My uncle fled to Sweden on skis.

When my paternal great-grandfather arrived in Minnesota in 1868, he was one of almost a million Norwegians who left for *Amerika* between 1820 and 1920, about a third of the country's population. Did he leave a shithole country? Few immigrants would use such a word to refer to home, no matter how dire their circumstances. My paternal grandparents were born in the States, but they spoke English with Norwegian accents all their lives, as did my father, a third-generation Norwegian American. They called it "a brogue." My grandparents never had indoor plumbing in the little house on the small farm they had to stop farming when they lost most of it during the Depression. The poverty and deprivation my father experienced growing up in that isolated rural immigrant community weighed heavily on him, a man who fought in World War II, went to college on the GI bill, met my mother at the University of Oslo in 1950, earned a PhD in Scandinavian studies, and became a scholar of his own people. He spent decades annotating an immense immigrant archive known as the Norwegian-American Historical Association.

Nativist madness is nothing new to the US, only the identity of the threatening immigrant Other changes. In 1844, New York's *Daily Plebeian* cited the "hordes of Dutch and Irish thieves and vagabonds, roaming about our streets." It railed against "English and Scotch pick-pockets and burglars [. . .] Italian and French mountebanks," and of course, the ever-suspicious "wandering Jews."

The Irish were depicted in the papers as subhuman apes, the Chinese as dangerous monsters. Race is a fiction made real by history. The slogan of the so-called Know Nothing movement: AMERICANS SHALL RULE AMERICA! Sound familiar? Who are we Americans? If your relatives weren't Native Americans or brought here on slave ships, are you not of immigrant stock? Are we a country built on amnesia?

When my mother gave birth to me in the hospital of our small Minnesota town, the nurses referred to her as "the foreign girl." I was "the foreign girl's baby." My mother discovered that the sight of her naked two-year-old on a beach in Wisconsin shocked the delicate, if oh-so-prurient sensibilities of midwesterners. In Norway all small children run naked in the sun. I was the only child in my grade school who ate sardine sandwiches for lunch. I sometimes mistook a Norwegian word for an English word and didn't realize my mistake until I confronted the blank face of a person with whom I had hoped to communicate. But I, the child of the foreign girl, learned what every offspring of immigration learns—double consciousness. The way things are here is not the way things are everywhere. There are words in my mother's tongue that have no equivalents in English. I can dance to different tunes. I am a creature of between here and there.

The grotesque ironies of the present are not lost on me. The grandson of immigrants and the husband of an immigrant rants about "shithole countries" in tones resonant of Nazi racial propaganda that described Jews, Black people, Roma people, homosexuals, epileptics, and the mentally handicapped as bacteria infecting the master race. Mexicans are rapists and Muslims must be banned, the president says. All Haitians have AIDS. A Jewish star sits beside a bag of money sits beside a picture of Hillary Clinton. Somalis in Maine are criminals. Sanctuary cities are "crime-infested breeding" grounds. "Very fine people," those neo-Nazis and KKK members in Charlottesville. *Don't let the animals in. Build a wall. The barbarians are at the gates.* In ancient Greece the barbarian was any foreigner who spoke a language incomprehensible to the natives. For the Greeks the Persians, the Phoenicians, the Egyptians, and the Celts were all ba-ba-ba babbling inferiors.

No, the hatred of the foreigner is nothing new. But some of us, the children and grandchildren and great-grandchildren of foreign girls and foreign boys, refuse to forget where we came from. We will not stand down. We will not be silent. And we will bark out and vote our alienation and outrage at the poisonous, xenophobic pollution fantasies and policies of the new regime. We will celebrate our differences and sing in our languages and share sardines and falafels and sambusas, and we will take to the streets. We are New Yorkers, after all, and we bump up against one another every day. Sometimes we bump and stick. Thirty-seven years ago, I married an American Jewish man from Brooklyn. We have a daughter. She calls herself a "Jewegian."

———————

SIRI HUSTVEDT is a novelist and scholar, who is the author of a book of poetry, seven novels, four collections of essays, and a work of nonfiction. She has a PhD in English literature from Columbia University and is a lecturer in psychiatry at Weill Cornell Medical College. Her scholarly work is interdisciplinary, and she has published papers in various academic and scientific journals. She is the recipient of numerous awards, including the International Gabarron Prize for Thought and Humanities (2012), the Los Angeles Book Prize for Fiction for *The Blazing World*, which was also long-listed for the Man Booker Prize (2015). In 2019, she won an Award for Literature from the American Academy of Arts and Letters, the European Essay Prize (Charles Veillon) for *The Delusions of Certainty*, a book-length essay on the mind/body problem, and the prestigious Princess of Asturias Award for Literature in Spain. She lives in Brooklyn, New York.

Finding Roots

A girl grapples with competing fantasies of Puerto Rico;
a family tale of leaving Vienna and finding vegetables and
love in Haiti; a novelist's formative years are experienced
as olfactory field recordings; a childhood reunion
onstage is accompanied by a harmonium; an artist
reflects on superheroes and the "Smack Express"

Stories by Sonia Manzano, Paul Holdengräber,
Tanaïs, DJ Tikka Masala, and Matt Huynh

Puerto Rico of My Dreams

BY SONIA MANZANO

The first time I saw my mother in the world she had come from, I was six. She was smiling at me from a black-and-white photo of herself in Puerto Rico. Posing in front of a run-down wooden shack with some bedraggled-looking children in the background, her smile was shy. Maybe because she felt self-conscious about the clothes she was wearing, a white suit with a peplum and spectator pumps on her feet, or because she was wearing such a beautiful outfit while standing in front of such a mean place.

I didn't know that the image of my elegantly dressed mother, standing in that impoverished setting, would come to represent my own relationship with Puerto Rico. That the image, seemingly in conflict with itself, would remind me of the Puerto Rico of my dreams, versus the Puerto Rico I would eventually visit.

When I first saw that photo, I had never been to Puerto Rico. And being raised at a time when children were rarely sincerely spoken to, I hungered for more knowledge about that place my parents had come from. The best way to get information was to listen, unobserved under the kitchen table. There I could catch any tiny glimpses of the island that my parents threw my way.

"My god, El Fanquito?" they'd exclaim with derision, describing a slum neighborhood referred to as "The Little Mud."

"Remember when the tide came in, children would drown in the sewage that ran beneath the houses?"

Children drowning in sewage? I imagined small children twirling their way down toilets and being flushed away. Puerto Rico, what a horrible place.

Sometimes I gleaned information from songs my parents sang. There was a song that told the tale of a *jibaro*, or peasant farmer, who had clawed vegetables out of the ground dreaming of the killing he'd make in town selling his goods. The lyrics bouncing on music fraught with emotion tell us he fails and is forced, yet again, to disappoint his starving family. The man was true and noble and I couldn't help but embrace the sadness of that tune. How heartbreakingly beautiful it was! How I wanted to meet more people like that *jibaro* in that song. How I wanted to *be* that *jibaro*. How proud I was to come from such noble stock. Some people had houses and cars that ran, and three full meals a day—but we Puerto Ricans, we had sad stories. What a dramatic place!

My desire for Puerto Rican stories was inadvertently satisfied by my fourth-grade elementary school teacher, Mr. Gitterman, when he said, "It's your mother's responsibility to read books to you."

I laughed at his suggestion. My overwhelmed mother, read stories to me? When was she going to do that? When she got home from slaving away all day at a dress factory? When every night, needing fortification for her evening shift at home, she'd brew coffee seconds after coming in the door. And after sitting for as long as it took a cupful of that sugary brew to slip down her throat, she'd get out of her stylish belted dress clothes and into her frumpy *bata* or house robe and get to work. Frying fatback to flavor the beans, boiling the water to cook the rice, yelling for my older sister to get out of her room and help her tend to me and my two younger brothers. She did all this while hoping my asthmatic brother wouldn't get an attack. And probably praying my father hadn't stopped off at a bar on his way home from work, stirring the devils inside him. Then my mother would have to drop everything to soothe his rage while protecting herself from his sudden fists.

Still, hearing a story was worth a shot. I brought it up while she was standing at the stove frying pork chops.

"My teacher says you have to read to me," I said.

"Paciencia!" she said stretching her hand up to the sky. When overwhelmed—which was all the time—my mother would ask God to give her patience. "Paciencia!" she'd vent, stretching her hands with such force and vigor, I thought for sure her fingers would someday dislodge God right off his throne. The pork fat sputtered in the pan to match the sparks emanating from her bug eyes. I suppressed a giggle.

"Don't I got enough to do?" she asked, triumphantly flipping a chop.

"That's what Mr. Gitterman said." I shrugged innocently.

"Tell your teacher we don't got any books!"

"You don't need books," Mr. Gitterman answered enthusiastically after I had related what Mami had said. "She can just tell you stories of her life!"

How lovely it would have been to hear stories as beautiful as the one in that song about the peasant! And to hear a story from my mother, the version of my mother who had stood in front of that shack in her peplum dress and pumps. What would she say? How would she say it?

She was scrubbing the oven when I brought it up.

She stopped. Her glance was noncommittal—but from that day on, there began a literary, word-of-mouth, slow reveal montage of her life in Puerto Rico.

"When I was little I could drink water from cascading waterfalls."

I let that sink in—water cascading just like that? That seemed impossible to me. Everyone knew water came out of faucets! All at once, there were colliding images in my head of faucets embedded in the rocks that my mother couldn't see because they were hidden by foliage. Was Puerto Rico a magical place?

Another time: "In Puerto Rico roosters sang us awake every morning." Sang? At the time, everybody was obsessed with Elvis Presley, so I conjured up images of roosters dressed as Elvis Presley.

And when she learned to drive she found time to tell me she remembered roads in Puerto Rico so curvy, and with so many sharp turns, you got goose bumps just riding on them. Thinking of goose bumps on Looney Toons cartoon characters, I visualized roads as dense with bumps as the goose bumps my own body produced when cold—with tiny cars navigating through them. Aha! So Puerto Rico was a funny place!

And then the sad stories of her mother dying. Of tuberculosis, she said—but between the lines I heard a more dramatic story. Of my grandfather, aptly named Dionysis Rivera, pressing his body against other women in sultry roadside bars as his wife, my saintly grandmother, Incarnacion Falcon, bore his five children. I see her ascending to heaven, broken heart exposed like Jesus's heart is exposed in photos of him in calendars.

And then, even more unhappy tales of my mother and her siblings being separated and distributed around, like indentured servants to whomever would have them so they could work for their room and board. I don't have to tell you this made me see Puerto Rico as a sad place.

But then she balanced the tales of woe with glorious narratives of herself as a young woman surviving hurricanes, of bravely crossing bull pens in order to visit a far-flung sibling. Her stories filled in the blanks of her personality.

What a place Puerto Rico must be! Full of drama, beauty, hatred, and love. All things Shakespearean, only in a hotter climate. Suddenly stories of children in sewers were forgotten and replaced with grander themes. I decided all things Puerto Rican were over-the-top, and I couldn't wait to get there. Surely the best things about being a Puerto Rican in New York were in abundance on the island. If we loved to eat roast pork shoulder at Christmas in the Bronx, in Puerto Rico, there must be people roasting pork in every corner of the island, at all times. If we, as good Catholics, ate *verdura* and bacalao dripping in olive oil on Fridays, there must be restaurants serving this food all day on Fridays in Puerto Rico.

The day of reckoning came when I finally visited at age fourteen. Would Puerto Rico be what I had dreamed of all these years?

It was not.

While I wanted to go into the mountains to drink from waterfalls, I was met by cousins who wanted to go to the movies. While I wanted to seek out musicians who played songs of noble *jíbaros*, my cousins wanted to iron their hair and go to the Condado Beach discos. Aunts and uncles who worked Monday through Friday at the utilities company were happy to grab dinner at a McDonald's on the way home. The islanders I met weren't so much old-timey *jibaro* farmers cultivating, then clawing vegetables out of the ground, but semi-professionals who got their vegetables in plastic wrap from supermarkets. Was I dismayed I was not met with the poverty my parents had endured?

Over the years I have visited Puerto Rico several times. My fantasy and reality never quite matching up, I'd come back to New York as if something was always just out of reach. Always with one foot in the past and one foot in the present. The Puerto Rico I was visiting just wasn't the same place I had grown up thinking about. Did I expect the island to stand still, like my mother in the photo, until I got there?

Years later, after reaching notoriety as Maria on *Sesame Street* I was asked to be the *madrina*, or godmother, in the annual Puerto Rican Day Parade in New York. Right before the parade's kickoff, a reporter from Puerto Rico asked me which town I represented. Self-conscious I hadn't been born on the island, I tried to be funny by saying, "I represent the Bronx!"

When he didn't laugh, I weakly added, "Sesame Street?"

Even that fell flat.

"Plaza Sesamo?" he asked, thinking of the Mexican version of *Sesame Street* that aired on the island. I started to explain the difference between the two shows when he interrupted me, earnestly asking, "What towns are your parents from?"

"Caguas and Manati!" I answered triumphantly. It was better than nothing.

The parade began. Balancing myself on the rim of the back seat of the convertible where I took my place as *madrina*, I looked at all the people along the parade route. People bursting with pride because they were Puerto Rican. Young men and women, and little kids who probably couldn't even pronounce "Puerto Rico," wearing red, white, and blue regalia inspired by the Puerto Rican flag. All cheering, wildly and joyously. Some of these people were third- and fourth-generation Puerto Ricans living in New York. I suspected some of them spoke even less Spanish than I did. Something told me many didn't have any relatives in Puerto Rico, or at least very few. I surmised that many might never have even been to the island. So what explained such a wild, tenacious cultural connection to Puerto Rico? Was it the bouquet of skin tones, hair types, and facial features that prompted us to celebrate so fiercely? Was it the diversity of race that made us all feel connected? Could that have been it?

Shortly after the parade I read an essay written by a Puerto Rican intellectual who lives on the island. He wrote that he didn't understand why mainlanders had to wrap themselves up in Puerto Rican flags and have such a showy event like the parade once a year, to prove who they were and what they loved. He said he felt Puerto Rican without the need for spectacle, or the wearing of T-shirts with the Puerto Rican flag for evidence.

I thought about why we celebrated so hard in that parade, at such breakneck speed. I wondered why we cheered so vociferously, we chanced choking on our own ethnicity. I decided that perhaps we mainlanders celebrated with such purpose and unity because we all yearned for the Puerto Rico of our dreams. The Puerto Rico that, like mine, we had fashioned after hearing stories from those who missed the island.

I don't know. But I do know that these collective dreams of Puerto Ricans on the mainland are big and have no boundaries. That they help us navigate realities here. The dreams serve as anchors or talismans to hold and protect us and allow us to grow. This ability to hang on to our roots, real or imagined, is a great strength. The Puerto Rico of our dreams, that is horrible, dramatic, magical, funny, sad, and glorious keeps us from drowning here. It helps us overcome and live our lives with a warm stone in our hearts.

That black-and-white photo of my elegantly dressed mother, standing in a poor locale, was not in conflict with itself after all. I was looking at the Puerto Rico of my dreams from the very beginning. It had been in front of me all the time!

SONIA MANZANO is a groundbreaking educator, executive television producer, actor, and award-winning children's book author. A first-generation mainland Puerto Rican, she has affected the lives of millions of parents and children since the early 1970s, when she was offered the opportunity to play Maria on *Sesame Street* (for which she received an Emmy Lifetime Achievement Award in 2016). In addition, Manzano has also received fifteen Emmys for writing television scripts, the Congressional Hispanic Caucus Award, and the Hispanic Heritage Award for Education. Her critically acclaimed children's books include *A World Together, No Dogs Allowed!*, *A Box Full of Kittens*, *Miracle on 133rd Street*, *The Revolution of Evelyn Serrano*, and the memoir *Becoming Maria: Love and Chaos in the South Bronx*. Her multibook deal with Scholastic was announced in 2020. Manzano, her husband, Richard, and their daughter, Gabriela, all reside in New York City.

Friendly Enemy Aliens

BY PAUL HOLDENGRÄBER

Thank you very much. I so much enjoy the fact that between every presentation, we clap. My father taught me how to clap really loudly. In 1933, he was a *claquette* in the opera house in Vienna. Because the Viennese public was so difficult, you needed about ten or twelve *claquettes* to rev up the crowd and make everybody appreciate the singers—even when they were terrible.

I suffer from a disease called "quotomania." I'm a quotomaniac by training, so from time to time, I'll quote different writers. So here is one quotation that matters greatly to me: "Don't limit a child to your own learning, for he is born in another time" from Rabindranath Tagore. There's a reason why I begin with that quotation. Because my parents, who were born in Vienna, gave me an incredible curiosity for life. Just before I went to university my father said to me: "Don't ever forget that the word *university* comes from the word *universe*, and the more interests you have, the more interesting you will be."

My parents left Vienna separately in 1938. My father, on the very last day you could leave, the fifteenth of June 1938, and my mother in April, a little bit earlier. My mother was then fourteen years old. My father had been a student in the Department of Medicine in Vienna, which he always said was the best department of medicine in the world—except for Montpellier (why Montpellier, I have never found out).

My parents didn't know each other in Vienna. They met once they were in Haiti. People often ask me, "Why Haiti?" and I always tell them that that question assumes agency. You went where you could go. There were a hundred and seven Jewish families in Haiti in 1938. There had been a very small Syrian Jewish community that lived in Haiti before the émigrés came. My father and mother, along with the other new arrivals, were given a particular denomination. They were "Friendly Enemy Aliens."

My father arrived on his own in Haiti with four dollars to his name. He was given a plot of land in Kenscoff, in the hills of Port-au-Prince, by the minister of agriculture. The minister believed that only a limited group of vegetables could be grown in the soil of Haiti. He gave my father a list of vegetables that had grown on the land before.

My father believed otherwise. He loved chemistry and, rather than being daunted by the limited list of vegetables the minister of agriculture submitted to him could grow on his small plot of land, he firmly believed he could grow all kinds of other vegetables too. So he went to the library of Port-au-Prince to read about soil, and he started to analyze his plot of land. From his reading and research, he came to suspect that the soil was similar to the soil of Senegal, where farmers had grown all kinds of different vegetables.

In his reading, he had come across Burpee, a seed company in Chicago. He sent a pound of soil to them and wrote a note. "Dear Burpee. My name is Kurt Holdengräber. I am a Friendly Enemy Alien. I have analyzed the soil of Kenscoff, near Port-au-Prince. I believe that the soil is very similar to the soil in Senegal. Could you tell me if I am right?" A month goes by, two months goes by, and on the third month he gets a huge box filled with seeds. The letter says "Dear Friendly Enemy Alien. We are Burpee, and we believe you are right. And good luck."

Of course, the first vegetables he grew he gave free of charge to the minister of agriculture. Eventually, he would distribute the remains of the day to some of the Jewish families, which is how he met my mother. She was sixteen when they met. My father would come to deliver vegetables, and my mother would serve tea, while my father played chess with my grandmother. He noticed my mother, she noticed him, they got married on September 26, 1943. She rented a dress and a ring. They were married for seventy-one years. And on the twenty-sixth of every month, my father would write down how many months they had been married. A very, very, very difficult act to follow—I would say, impossible.

Forty years after my parents arrived in Kenscoff, I ask my father if we can go to Haiti together. So my father and mother and sister and I all go to Haiti. And we are looking at these extraordinary farm stands, and my father is showing me the vegetables. We are seeing these vegetables that had never grown here before my father planted them.

And he says, "You see, Pauli? This is my legacy."

So I say to him, "Daddy, we have to write a book together."

And he says, "No, no, no. I live it, you write it."

My father was fairly disappointed (he didn't say it, but I knew he was) because I wasn't studying medicine, or anything useful, but he somewhat admired the choice of philosophy. That day, when he sat me down before I was off to study philosophy at the Université Catholique de Louvain, in Belgium, he said, "You'll be reading a lot about the soul, and about the meaning of life, and that is very important. But don't forget to cross the street." What he was alluding to was that in Vienna the medical school was across the street from the philosophy school. He said, "You need to cross the street, go to the anatomy class, and see how they cut bodies open. You need to look at the heart and soul, but from a different perspective."

When I hurt my finger opening an envelope, I nearly faint. Seeing a little bit of blood is terrifying to me. So I never really crossed the street, but in effect, I would say that the idea of "crossing the street," the idea of translation, of moving from one world to another inhabits my whole life.

When I worked at the New York Public Library hosting the LIVE from NYPL series, I spoke to people from all walks of life and I think that, to some extent, that form of moving from one world to the other—the way my parents had to move from one world to the other—inhabits me, and helps me greatly.

I think my time is more or less up, alas. Let me leave you with the beginning of a poem I love, by a poet I love, the Palestinian American poet Naomi Shihab Nye.

RED BROCADE

The Arabs used to say,
When a stranger appears at your door,
feed him for three days
before asking who he is,
where he's come from,
where he's headed.
That way, he'll have strength
enough to answer.
Or, by then you'll be

such good friends
you don't care.
Let's go back to that.
Rice? Pine nuts?
Here, take the red brocade pillow.
My child will serve water
to your horse.

Note: This piece represents an individual perspective and the author's memories of his father. It does not aim to represent Haiti's complex history or its people.

PAUL HOLDENGRÄBER is an interviewer and curator. He is the founding executive director of Onassis Los Angeles, a center for dialogue. Since March 2020, he has been the creator and host of *The Quarantine Tapes*, a daily podcast copresented by Dublab and Onassis LA (https://quarantine-tapes.simplecast.com). Previously, and for fourteen years, he was the founder and director of the New York Public Library's LIVE from the NYPL cultural series where he interviewed and hosted over six hundred events, holding conversations with everyone from Patti Smith to Zadie Smith, Ricky Jay to Jay-Z, Errol Morris to Jan Morris, Wes Anderson to Helen Mirren, Werner Herzog to Mike Tyson. Before his tenure at the library, Holdengräber was the founder and director of The Institute for Arts & Culture at the Los Angeles County Museum of Art, and a Fellow at the Getty Research Institute in Los Angeles. He has a PhD in comparative literature from Princeton University and has taught at Princeton University, Williams College, Claremont Graduate University, among others. In 2003, the French government named Holdengräber Chevalier des Arts et des Lettres and then promoted him in 2012 to the rank of Commandeur des Arts et des Lettres. In 2010, the president of Austria awarded him the Austrian Cross of Honor for Science and Art.

Field Notes from My Youth

BY TANAÏS

Alabama & Missouri/Scent: Jasmine & Butter

I consider the years before I became a novelist or perfumer as one long olfactory field recording. In my notebooks there are written fragments of scent memories, each illuminating a specific place and season and a sense of yearning, where scents are akin to comfort, a sense of place, a way to fit in where I do not belong.

The women in my family wore perfumes they'd heard of back home in Bangladesh, coveted and displayed proudly on dressers when they came to own them. Throughout my childhood, we ping-ponged across the country: Illinois, where I was born, on to Texas, Alabama, Missouri. My father struggled to find steady work as a chemist, while my mother in typical Bangladeshi hustler fashion worked in fashion boutiques, movie theaters, and grocery stores and got her bachelor's degree in geography. Nina Ricci L'Air du Temps stood exalted on my mother's dresser in a tiny Missouri apartment. The frosted glass doves on the bottle's cap exuded aspirations of elegance and wealth she coveted from the tiny apartments that dotted my childhood across the Midwest and South. The ornate bottle looked sad in its surroundings, just like my mother's gold and saris hanging in the dingy closet they lived inside. On nights Ma worked concessions at the movie theater, my sister and I rubbed her feet, scented with buttery popcorn and faded perfume.

My grandmother lived with us throughout the years, even becoming a US citizen before her children, who'd helped bring her to the States. She wore attar of jasmine, a narcotic floral with an animal stink. She was forever a village girl. Loved a swim in the pond and bright red lipstick on special occasions. She lived between her children's homes, becoming a caretaker for her grandchildren, a portal into our motherland. I suffered bouts of pneumonia as a kid, which required nasty, nauseating medicine. One morning, when I couldn't stop throwing up, my grandmother dipped a pair of cotton balls in her jasmine attar and tucked them into my ears. I lay with my head on her lap, until the scent lulled me to sleep. Perfume as escape, as pleasure, as lineage, as matriarchy.

I don't recall the feeling of my mother language fading away when I learned English. I remember watching *Good Times* or *Facts of Life* and understanding the people on TV but not speaking much English. I began kindergarten in Auburn, Alabama, a land of football fanatics and very few Bangladeshis. Being a scrawny child with a whispery voice made me the target of a young Persian girl who bullied me in benign ways that cut me—telling me the obvious fact I was dark, making sure I knew I was ugly. We were neither

Black, nor white like our classmates; in a census, her people, Persians, would be, and still are, counted as white. I was too stupid to jump rope, too dirty to hold her show-and-tell doll. We didn't know then that as adults we'd be seen as the same enemy.

The next year, we moved to Missouri. I enrolled in the Robert E. Lee Elementary School. Each month, students were selected as Patriots of the Month, rather than the more typical Student of the Month or Honor Roll. We won a red, white, and blue flag embroidered with Confederate stars. I coveted that ribbon, a five-year-old ignorant of its violent racist history. My teacher loved dusting crumbs of those orange peanut butter crackers all about her classroom. At that point I'd only known English for a couple of years, so I felt shy to speak it. She was convinced I didn't speak the language at all. In Missouri 1988, most Americans I interacted with—my teacher and classmates—had never even heard of Bangladesh, which had become a country in 1971. Well, my father marched into the school when he saw her notes on a report card. He was livid. I'd been reading in fucking English for the last two years, he thundered, this teacher was racist. To appease him, the principal let him do a presentation about Bangladeshi culture for my class, which somehow led to my classmates' respect for our land of pretty fabric and slow music and palm trees and river boats. I remember the surreal feeling of having the line between my private Bangla self bleed into my American school self—and having my friends think of where we came from as captivating.

By the time the Gulf War began a few years later, I learned to bear the burden of my given name, Tanwi Nandini Islam, of being an Islam in America. On one hand, proud of being Bangladeshi, on the other, hiding my last name from potentially psychotic white folks. During the war (Is there ever a time that's not "during the war"?) a regular Saturday trip to the farmers' market meant encountering Islamophobic T-shirts sold by friendly white farmers, right alongside their berries. One shirt screamed HUSSEIN IS INSANE! over a demonic Saddam's face. Sometimes I wonder if these same people have switched over to Make America Great Again snapbacks. And when I think of the principal's small concession to my father, it's just another instance of white folks expecting that we teach them that our existence matters. More than thirty years later, I wish I could say this has changed, but September 11 calcified the Islamophobia of my youth into endless war in Iraq and Afghanistan, xenophobic attacks against Sikhs and Muslims, and a general consensus that Islam is inherently violent—erasing the millions upon millions of Muslims who disavow all forms of violence.

New York/Scent: Turmeric, Coconut, Tropical Fruits, Smoke

I consider myself a New Yorker. I came here when I was ten years old. I hit puberty here. I became obsessed with being cool here. No matter how many candles we lit or air fresheners we spritzed, the sizzle of those spices clung to the walls of our house, our skin, our hair. I spent my hard-earned money from working a retail job at the mall on clothes, cigarettes, and smelling like the tropics, Victoria's Secret spritzes and fancy coconut-floral shampoos and conditioners that flattened my wavy black hair as well as they erased the sharp scent of curry.

I was in a troubled, tumultuous relationship with an Indian Christian boy who slathered himself in Issey Miyake and worked at Burger King. A few months of dating the guy and I started calling myself Indian. It seemed like a victimless lie.

"What are you wearing? Take that thing off. You're a Muslim!" my mother snapped when she caught the glint of my boyfriend's cross on my neck. Of course, where I saw love, my mother saw sin. I left the tiny Jesus on my neck, feeling the cool metal on my chest, a reminder that a simple piece of jewelry could change me. I coveted the unburdened secularity of my Indian Christian friends. They could drink, date, eat pork, or wear short skirts. For my parents, my rejection of myself as Bangladeshi or as Muslim was a slap in the face. They'd survived a war where millions of people died just so I could be that. That they've always held on to Islam as a source of strength, through war, immigration, financial distress, and family death is now a part of my own spiritual practice. Whereas back then I felt shame and restriction, today, I've returned to my family's faith, fasting for Ramadan and building artistic communities with Muslims across the diaspora.

When my boyfriend brought up conversion and church talk, I stopped wearing the cross. His last gift to me was a bottle of Elizabeth Taylor's White Diamonds. He'd put in a lot of drive-through shifts to buy it. I sprayed myself with the perfume and hid it deep in my drawer, but my mother sniffed my lies (and my deflowering) every time I walked by. I'd leave our hookups in the local park smelling like a smoky old woman. In some way, our perfumes let us transcend a dead-end relationship in the suburbs. We were not meant to be together, but we shared the same quest: to find a scent that would mask the smell of where we came from.

TANAÏS (née Tanwi Nandini Islam) is the New York–based author of the critically acclaimed novel *Bright Lines* (Penguin 2015), which was a finalist for the Center for Fiction First Novel Prize, Edmund White Debut Fiction Award, and the Brooklyn Eagles Literary Prize. Tanaïs is the founder of TANAÏS, a beauty, fragrance, and design studio in New York City, and is currently at work on their forthcoming book *In Sensorium: Notes for My People*, a lyric essay collection blending memoir and theory on scent, sensuality, South Asian and Muslim perfume cultures, colonization, and its aftermath.

Where Did We Go?

BY DJ TIKKA MASALA

So this is what happened. I had a gig at Henrietta Hudson, the bar I DJ at. It was the oldest, and longest-standing lesbian bar in the country at that time, in 2018. My team there was typically a scrappy, gritty crew of immigrant queers, native New Yorkers, and nightlife veterans. Our regulars on Thursdays consisted of locals from the five boroughs, and the occasional tourist. The music ranged between hip-hop, reggaetón, and pop. It was a little bit like moving the radio dial between Hot 97 and La Mega, plus some Bollywood and global dance music from me. The soundtrack traveled between the '90s and the moment. It was an inherently intergenerational crowd, so it made sense as a multicultural, local, and international throwback night. At the end of the gig I grabbed a cab to get home. The driver was Bengali, I could tell by his name.

We started up a conversation and it came up that I also am Bengali. This was interesting to him, because he had assumed that I was a Puerto Rican dyke, because usually Bengali women don't dress like me, or have hair like mine, or have my particular gender expression, which is neither here nor there. He surprised me by being more curious than judgmental and we found ease in sharing our stories about family and music.

He told me about his life in Bangladesh, and the hours he worked to send money home. I told him about my family, in Kolkata. I told him that I was disconnected from them, except for my younger brother and our cousin. The family had separated several times over, and for different reasons over the years. Healing or hiding from these rifts was an ongoing, lifelong process that for me involved music as a healer. I told him my family's claim to fame was in building harmoniums. His eyes widened in the rearview mirror at the mention of Pakrashi Harmonium.

The harmonium is an instrument that came to India from Europe, as a seated organ with a foot pump for pressing air through the interior chambers. It was adapted for the floor-seated styles of performing Indian songs. At the end of its transformation the air flows through a series of precisely cut metal pieces, much like the way a harmonica works, except the metal resonating through wood makes for a distinctive tone and timbre, which emanates through the ornately carved top. The length of each piece of metal determines what note plays through it.

When the instrument first started being used in Indian classical music, purists denounced it because it couldn't play microtones, the notes between the notes, required for comprehensive accompaniment. It was never meant to be a traditional solo instrument, it was a portmanteau, and looked like a large wooden suitcase. It is a combination of separate parts that create a new meaning in their unity, out of wood and metal, wind and keys, east and west. Pakrashi Harmonium started building these in 1923, when India's film industry was located in Kolkata. Their factory consisted of multigenerational craftsmen, masters and their apprentices, building models to order using building techniques honed over generations. My harmonium was built under my uncle's direction, and I've had it since childhood. My first music teacher told me that one must play this instrument regularly or the sound would lose its suppleness because it is a living breathing object.

The cabdriver told me he had one of my family's instruments in his mom's house. I told him I grew up studying Indian vocal classical music, but that I stopped singing a long time ago. And that's when he said he missed his mother's voice, and her singing, and that it would make his night if someone from my family sang him a song, so I agreed. Mind you, I am terrified of singing as an adult. I chose a song called "Purano Shei Diner Kosha," which every Bengali knows, and told him I might need some backup, so he sang along. By the end of it we were both emotional, missing our families and the land we came from. He had turned his meter off somewhere on the Manhattan Bridge while the skyline passed out of our peripheral vision. It was suddenly a free ride home from a stranger in tears.

The next day I made a social media post about what happened, and my friend Sofija reached out to me and asked if I would sing the song at her show, This Alien Nation. Remember the part where I'm afraid of singing? I asked if I could bring a friend along to sing it for me, and that I would tell the story of the cab ride, and translate the song. I knew exactly who would sing it.

I was always intimidated by Rini, because she had a voice that was a gift from the universe. Our parents were friends.

They had landed in New Jersey in the '80s and met at Durga Puja, the major seasonal holiday gathering the Bengalis in New Jersey organized. Most Hindu Bengalis are part of the tradition of Shaktism, which involves worshipping powerful Mother Goddesses, like Kali, Durga, Saraswati, and Lakshmi. There are a few male costars sprinkled around the pantheon, but it's unquestionably centered around the divine feminine. Our families worshipped many goddesses, while the world around us was monotheistically orbiting a masculine power, God or his son, Jesus.

I heard Rini sing the first time when we were six and learned at that age that there's a big difference between a gifted musician, and someone who was getting by. Our parents put us in music lessons when we were thirteen. There was an understanding that our Sundays were for Indian music, and that our friends at school wouldn't have the tools to conceptualize the whole story of why.

It was intimidating to be in class with Rini every Sunday. She cultivated abundant talent with self-discipline, and I just had a lot of work to do. I never felt prepared, but I did my best with what I had. Rini and I had a demanding superstar teacher who was a powerhouse performer, and strict.

The year we were off to college, music lessons stopped. I went to Rutgers, and Rini took a year off to be with her mom, who was battling cancer. Her mother always made me feel special, and seen; she was an empath, and kind. In college my Sundays were no longer about Indian music, they were about recovering from Saturday nights with a newfound queer chosen family. Being a queer Bengali was not easy at that time, my family didn't know what to do with this identity or where it placed in sustaining tradition in a culturally alien American reality. In my case it created an irreparable rift with my parents after I came out at seventeen, when my mom walked in on a first kiss with my big high school crush. Everything changed after that.

My second year in college I took a resident adviser job. Halfway through the year my supervisor let me know that a new resident was entering the dorms. It was Rini. Her mom had passed, she was starting college, and I was going to be her RA. So much had changed, and we were comforted to see each other again. My friends became her friends, and we looked out for each other. It was healing for me to have a Bengali friend, without being judged. I was an activist on campus, and my queer life and dorm life were like having a dual identity, which I drifted deeper into as time passed. Rini and I lost touch after college, but she was the person who I immediately thought of for this performance—I wanted to hear her sing this song.

After Sofija got in touch, I looked for Rini online—I was sure she'd still be singing somewhere out there. After finding a track by her on SoundCloud, I used the contact info there to reach her. It was a thrill to hear back, and it felt as if no time had passed. She agreed to sing onstage and we talked for the first time in fifteen years. It felt like discovering a time capsule. We agreed to share our story, I would bring my harmonium and she would play it and sing the song.

We reunited in the green room of Joe's Pub, a hallowed ground for the world's musical talent. It was an intimidating roster of readers, and we were honored to share that stage. It was an extraordinary moment for us; it was a chance to go beyond the music and tell our story of migration, transformation, loss and recovery of self. Her husband was a professional musician who frequented Joe's stage, but this would be a first for her. He was home taking care of their new baby. Rini was a new mother and made time in the midst of a high-priority care schedule to make space for this show. I told her that I became a DJ as a side gig through grad school and hadn't stopped, and that, yes, I wrote music for feminist acrobats. My brother was born the month after 9/11, just after I became her RA. I told her he was taller than me now, had figured out how to find me, rebelling against our mother, for love's sake.

We could have talked all night, but it was time to take the stage. We worked out the order of things, warmed up on the instrument, and decided we'd both talk some, she would perform, and at the end I would translate the song from Bengali to English.

After that my mind, flooding with panic, anxiety-drifted right into the reeds of the harmonium, worrying about whether everything was tightened correctly. I wondered if the pressure on the bellow was going to be okay for Rini, I knew she hadn't played in a while. It's a wind instrument with a keyboard, so a lot can go wrong if you don't get to practice with how the thing breathes, or how stiff or loose the keys are. The whole thing is made with hand-carved pieces of wood, and metal, so it sounds different with humidity and heat. The conditions of the room it's in directly influence its sound, every time.

What if the heat made the wooden keys expand and stick to each other? Where was the sheet with the song translation on it? Did we both have bottles of water? I'm pretty sure I tightened the resonators enough but not too much? Was this the right microphone for this instrument? Was she worrying about her new baby, at home right now?

I put on a smile, flattened out the paper, and put it on the surface of the harmonium, which has my last name carved into it, right across the top. If you look under the hood, at the reed bed, the person who cut each of the metal pieces that create that iconic sound also has his name hammered into the metal in block letters. In this way the artist marks their work; R. Mistry had built mine, and you can tell when it was built between 1923 and the moment by the factory's archive.

My harmonium was built in the early '90s. Rini told the audience my family was like the Stradivarius of harmoniums, and I remembered the year I got that harmonium after a trip to Kolkata with my family when I was a young teenager. I got to see the factory, and the rows of seasoned craftsmen, seated on the floor, carving reeds, wooden parts, in what felt like an ancient assembly line. They kept their eyes on the work and barely noticed me walking through behind my uncle, a tall handsome man with gray hair and sharp features, who looked like an older version of my father.

Rini and I stepped out onto the stage. When you're on a microphone at Joe's Pub, you know New York understands you. You know, on some level, that the culture of the city is acknowledging your existence and life experience. New York City is arguably the immigrant capital of the world. It can argue with Kolkata for that though. Pride aside, my hands were shaking, trying to hold the piece of paper with the song translation and the social media post that got us to that stage on it. My eyes kept returning to my last name carved out on the instrument's polished, almost brown burgundy, wood surface. It's amazing what a series of words or letters can do.

I scanned the rows for my friends in the audience. My crew was sitting in a row, beaming with attentive tenderness. Each of these women were immigrants born in other countries and making it happen for themselves here. They sat like a proud counsel of migrant siblings, they treated me like a star. A star who works all night and gets home when most people are about to wake up. I felt them holding me as the adrenaline escalated. Sitting next to this miraculous artist I studied next to for so long, and on such a lofty stage, helped with momentum.

In the audience I also saw Rini's father's face watching us. I remembered so many performances as a young person, where our parents sat in a row together, observing our progress intently. They were a jury with critical feedback every time, that kept feeding us, and pushing us to stick to it. They kept us in classes so we wouldn't lose our grip on understanding the beauty of our origins, our families' culture, and our language. If we were learning to sing this music, we were also learning to understand, interpret, and pronounce this music. This was their gift to us as children, and despite the rifts of cultural adaptation, I always felt like I belonged inside of Indian music somewhere.

I told the audience how Rini and I had arrived on that stage. Rini talked about music lessons when we were kids, and what it felt like to be preserving our heritage on the weekends while also trying to fit in. It was bittersweet.

Then it was Rini's turn to sing while backing herself up on harmonium. Her left hand pulled air into the instrument, while the right released notes into the air with deft keystrokes. The harmonium sounded like an instrument from another time, one that used wood and metal to saturate the air with the resonance of adaptation and resilience.

Her voice carried the words to the audience in our precious Bangla, but to the tune of "Auld Lang Syne." After the final diminuendo I gave the translation I'd written. I could see eyes watering among my friends and loved ones there.

Bengali:

Purano sei diner katha bhulbi kire haay.
O shei chhokher dekha, praaner katha, se ki bhola jaay.
Aay aar-ektibar aay re sakha, praaner maajhe aay.
Mora sukher dukher katha kabo, praan jurabe taay.
Mora bhorer bela phul tulechhi, dulechhi dolaay—
Baajiye bnaashi gaan geyechhi bokuler talaay.
Haay maajhe holo chhaarachhaari, gelem ke kothaay—
Aabar dekha jodi holo sakha praaner maajhe aay.

English:

How could you forget about our times together that have
    passed?
Is it possible to forget how we saw each other or how we
    spoke from our souls?
Friend, please return to me once again.
Let us talk about our joy and grief.
Let us find peace together.
We used to pick flowers early in the morning, and would
    play on the swing.
We would play the flute, and sing in the shades of the
    Bakul tree.
We scattered ourselves and lost touch, where did we go?
But if and when we reunite, I invite you into my heart.

———————

DJ TIKKA MASALA is a Brooklyn-based DJ, producer, and artist, originally from Kolkata, India, and raised in New Jersey. She is resident DJ at the historical Henrietta Hudson, the oldest lesbian bar in the country, where she has been throwing Homotown, which was listed on the *New York Times* roundup of the top ten party nights for queer women, in their *Pride: 50 Years of Parades and Protests* collection. She has DJed all over the world, including the Obama White House in 2010. She started producing and composing music for the Obie and Bessie award-winning feminist acrobatic company, LAVA Brooklyn, in 2011. Since 2018 Tikka has been on the NYC Mayor's Office's Nightlife Advisory Board, which interfaces between the worlds of nightlife and public policy. By day Tikka is the communications department for the Audre Lorde Project, an iconic movement education and organizing center for Queer People of Color in NYC.

Leaving Cabramatta

BY MATT HUYNH

The last time I went back home to Sydney, a guy in a bar sneezed, looked over, and said to me, "I guess I'm allergic to Chinese."

I wanted to tell him: *But I'm not Chinese, not really. Maybe half Chinese, and that's if you added up the quarters from a little further back in my family history. But I don't really have any connection to my Chinese ancestry. I'm more Vietnamese. But only because of my last name, and my face. I don't speak any Vietnamese. I was born in Australia. But I grew up surrounded by Vietnamese people. But I've never been to Vietnam, I spent my whole childhood in Australia, but no one asks me about the Australian experience, even though it's the only thing I've known.*

It just seemed too much effort. I don't think he cared, really. So I just laughed it off—like I was in on the joke on myself. Finished my drink. Told myself it didn't matter. I hated that it didn't matter. That explaining myself was too much of a bother.

My parents were refugees from the Vietnam War. After the Fall of Saigon, with my brothers (who were one year old and three months old), they fled on boats, escaped pirates, and waited in a Malaysian refugee camp for two years until they were resettled in Australia, where I was born.

I grew up in a suburb called Cabramatta, where migrant hostels had been located since World War II. New arrivals would be directed there for temporary accommodation in re-purposed army huts. As migrants resettled from the hostels into the surrounding area, the community's composition changed, according to the international conflict of the moment. At various times it was Italian, Yugoslavian, Polish, and Lebanese. But the Cabramatta I grew up in, after the Vietnam War, was heavily populated by immigrants from Vietnam, China, Cambodia, and Laos.

Australia had only just formally ended its racist "White Australia Policy" in the 1970s. The policy was a series of laws designed to exclude nonwhite immigration to Australia since Federation, the birth of the Australian Nation. When my family arrived, Australia—emerging from decades of xeno-phobic ideology—was ill-equipped to support migrants of color. Communities like ours bore the brunt of Australia's "multicultural experiment" where "multiculturalism" largely meant assimilation and integration, while at the same time isolating communities of migrants in enclaves without ade-quate infrastructure, social support, translators, or commu-nity services. But ours was a community of survivors.

People would borrow and raise money through neighbor-hood banking pools that operated out of homes and garages, so they could avoid banks, which felt impossible to deal with without recognized accreditation, jobs, or language skills. People pooled for private security for businesses, and orga-nized groups to walk to work together. Some of my friends' parents sewed clothes for sweatshop rates in their garages for clothing stores they'd be uncomfortable entering.

People found other ways to survive, too. When I was growing up, 5T was the most notorious Vietnamese gang in Cabramatta. The kids in the gang were really young, ranging from fourteen to their early twenties. Pocked with needle marks from tattoos and drugs, draped in microfiber shirts, baby faces framed by licks of highlighted hair blasted with synthetic sun. They had a grip over the community. They committed home invasions, ran protection rackets, and became known for turning our off-the-beaten-track suburban neighborhood into Australia's heroin capital.

The 5T gang was so-called after five Vietnamese words starting with the letter *T*. The news would say it meant: "love, money, prison, punishment, revenge." It also roughly translated to the Vietnamese words for "childhood without love." These were children abandoned by a generation of parents who themselves felt abandoned by their new community and their government. The parents were too young, too ill-equipped, too busy scraping by to know how to parent, trying to bridge a language and cultural barrier with their own kids.

Our local representative went on TV to say that "the Asian gangs don't fear our laws. But there's one thing they do fear, and it's possible deportation back to the jungles of Vietnam. Because that's, quite frankly, where they belong." When he was murdered in his driveway, he became Australia's first political assassination. Some of the local shops shut in a show of respect. A year later, 5T's gang leader was executed, and again, some of the local shops shut out of a show of respect.

I saw the train station as the very limit of our little world. Because my parents didn't let my siblings and me spend time there, but also because it was the way out of Cabramatta. When I was a kid, I'd fantasize, not just about getting on the train and running away from home, but flying away. I loved larger-than-life wrestlers, pop stars, superheroes. Just before starting kindergarten, I'd asked Ma to draw Superman for me. I loved watching anyone draw, because it was something I wished I could do myself. I could barely make the connection that behind these pulpy artifacts recording monsters and superheroes was a human hand, and that it could be mine. It was an act of magic. Ma grew up drawing ethereal Vietnamese girls in long dresses with a line so graceful and so deliberate, it felt like her marks were forever waiting to land on the page. My brother came home from school to find me in a crying fit because she had given Superman an elegant, pointed chin and long, delicate fingers in flaky, crumbly crayon. I sobbed to my brother, "Superman is not a 'crayon' character. He's marker." He told me to draw it myself. So I started drawing. I'd draw and write my way out of reality. I'd get lost in stories about indestructible men who zipped above ordinary people like me and dropped into our lives to anonymously perform uncelebrated acts of bravery, protect us, and disappear again in daylight. The superheroes that were as far from me as New York was from Cabramatta. I'd trace over them with a ballpoint pen and a heavy hand, digging myself deeper into the pages until they were unrecognizable under the pressure.

We'd do our weekly grocery shopping across the road from the train station, where there was a row of markets, bakeries, butchers, a doctor, a hardware store, and a newsagent, and we'd spot the junkies come off the trains to be quickly greeted by knowing looks from dealers.

It takes almost an hour to get to my neighborhood from the city center by train, but waves of drug tourists would choose that ride over visiting King's Cross, Sydney's red-light district, because they believed the heroin in Cabramatta was cheaper and purer. The news called the train to Cabramatta the "Smack Express." I can remember when there were still flower beds at the station. Sprinkled with glittering foil packages, buried like stars in the dirt.

My parents didn't need to lecture us about keeping away from the train station. We understood it would be offensive to the gravity they stressed on our studies. Their message was clear from the fact that they wouldn't even answer the phone. If visiting friends and having guests were a threat or, at best, an inconvenience, where would it be worth catching a train to? To parents who were raising children and escaping war since they were nineteen, what did "hanging out" even mean? I knew better.

My parents' way of showing my siblings and me they loved us was to protect us. To keep us fed, clothed, and sheltered. As much as they could, they kept an eye on us between repairing cars, working on assembly lines, and driving forklifts. Like many of my friends' families, we were taught to be grateful for what we had, to not attract attention, keep our heads down, keep to ourselves. The curtains and shades in my house were kept drawn. Every door had a number of locks on both the outside and the inside. As though we were keeping ourselves in from the world as much as we were keeping it out.

But we had a rich life inside. My parents paid special care to the back garden—what we called the space between the back screen-door and the factory wall behind us. We grew an abundance of practical plants: aloe vera, a pair of lemon trees, aromatics, leafy greens, and chili plants.

The only plant Ma kept for its purely useless gratuitous beauty was one that reminded her of her home country. It was called "Quynh," or "Queen of the Night." Ma would wake me in the single night of the year that the cactus flowered to share it like a secret. Its buds would grow to reveal smaller petals, opening again to reveal stems, and tinier buds, the flower would fill the night with its strong perfume, and die. Its entire life would arrive and leave in the space of a few hours, once a year, and only ever in the night. Ma tried telling me a poem about it, but I wasn't interested back then. Witnessing the Queen of the Night was intense for Ma, like she was reaching for a dream or a memory, whilst resigned to its inevitable departure in ordinary daylight.

I found an old composition book Ma kept in the two years my family spent in the refugee camp. Every line is packed tight with her Vietnamese script without any pauses or breaks. She told me that if you read it the right way up, they were recipes for meals she couldn't cook while in the camp. And if you turned it back to front, they were lyrics to songs she could only hear inside her head.

I finally got to leave Cabramatta each day, by taking the Smack Express, to go in the opposite direction. I would travel into the city to go to law school. It was everything my parents wanted for me. But I always kept drawing, folding, and stapling my own comics and giving them away to anyone who'd look at them.

I had the opportunity to leave Cabramatta because of everything my parents did to protect us. But concentrating on schoolwork and sticking to my Asian migrant microcosm had insulated me from the world, and from racism—until I was surrounded by rich white kids. Whether it was a joke or a sneeze, a judgmental look or lazy assumption, it betrayed how they saw me: because of where I was from, or looked like I was from. I was getting my fancy "official" degree and getting on that train out of Cabramatta, but I'd never be able to leave it behind.

As I entered my final year of law school, I bristled at the

thought of those bachelor of law letters, "LLB," stamped after my own name. I walked out of a class not knowing what I wanted to do with my life, except that I couldn't do law and quickly realizing that I couldn't do much else except draw.

Everything from my first commission to my first exhibition felt like I had pulled a fast one over everyone. I'd never been to art school, didn't have any mentors, didn't know anyone else who was working in a creative industry. I had never even stepped into a gallery until I left high school. I decided that I'd better take my dreams as far as I could go, because someone like me, someone who came from where I came from, wasn't ever meant to make it this far.

In those stories that I'd obsessed over of indestructible, flying men, New York was where they all lived and worked. But when I was a kid, it felt just as realistic to make art as it was to fly and bounce bullets off my chest. Part of me feels just as defiant and brave as those superheroes for dedicating myself to a life I only dreamt of as a kid, for making my own way into cities I only imagined in four-colored panels, for building my own home, from my own choices. But another part of me feels crestfallen—that I felt like I had to leave to be able to do so. That I'm just running away again.

My parents ran away from war, communists, reeducation camps, pirates. As far as they are concerned, I ran away to New York to draw funny pictures. But even though my fascination with comics sprung from wishing I could change my identity and escape my insular life in Cabramatta, when it came to making my own comics, I was obsessed with telling stories of the people and places I felt were unseen and unspoken for. Beside heroes in capes protecting sprawling metropolises on the comic book spinner rack, I wanted to see stories of people like my friends and family growing up in places like

Cabramatta. Escaping war, building new homes, and inventing personal formulations of family in alien lands.

Sometimes, someone will tell me I am doing "important work." How I make sense of that is that I assume my art makes them feel the same way I do—the same haunted curiosity, confusion, doubt, and evasive generational memories I'm reaching and grasping after. Making art—animation, comics, storytelling, telling this story now—has let me look back more directly and clearly than I could on my own. And maybe it helps other people too.

But I wonder if they feel as selfish as I do. To be poking and prodding and playing with old bruises. Not just my bruises, but sore spots for my community, my loved ones.

At the airport, Ma tells me to eat right, for the millionth time.

For the first time I can remember, my parents tell me they love me—clearly and in English, too.

For the first time since I was a baby, Ba hugs me.

And for the first time, they let me go.

MATT HUYNH is a Vietnamese-Australian visual artist and storyteller. His brush-and-ink paintings are informed by calligraphic Eastern sumi-e ink traditions and popular Western comic books. His work interrogates the vast repercussions of war, with a particular focus on amplifying diasporic voices, telling refugee narratives and the experiences of asylum seekers and migrant communities. Huynh's animations, comics, and murals have been exhibited by the MoMA, the Smithsonian, and the New-York Historical Society. His work has been honored by the Eisners, Pulitzer, and World Illustration Awards. Huynh lives and works in New York City.

Acknowledgments

Thank you to the contributors. For your talent and your kindness. Articulating one's life for an audience is difficult and doing so is an act of generosity. I am honored that you shared your stories.

To those who made this book happen. A very big thank-you to my agent, Marya Spence at Janklow and Nesbit—for your love of this project and your continued support. I'm very lucky to have you. Many thanks to the excellent Natalie Edwards. And to Michael Steger—for your expertise, guidance, and patience.

Judith Curr at HarperOne, thank you for your unwavering encouragement, your dedication to amplifying new voices, and your work in changing the publishing landscape. Thank you to the wonderful Rosie Black for seeing this project through. Thanks to the talented team at HarperVia, including Mary Grangeia, Yvonne Chan, Stephen Brayda, Alicia Tatone, Ralph Fowler, Ashley Yepsen, Courtney Nobile, Alison Cerri, Liat Kaplan, Maya Lewis, and Andrew Jacobs.

Thank you to Matt Huynh for your art and friendship.

This book stemmed from our live show. Thank you to Michaela McGuire (Programmer-at-large) and Trish Nelson (Producer), who started it with me. None of this would have been possible without you. Thank you for your hard work, and dedication to immigrant voices, and for your friendship. Shannon Manning who joined us as producer—thank you for the love you give to your work, and for evolving the show (wildcards!).

Thank you to Alex Knowlton and the staff at Joe's Pub for your continued support, for letting us make New York's best stage our home.

Thank you to all the guests who honored our stage and shared immigration stories, which couldn't all fit in one book. Thank you to those wonderful people in our audience.

Thank you to Payton Turner for the beautiful artwork for our live show, and for supporting us from the start.

Many thanks to the talented photographers Justin Wee, Helen Melville, Kat Burdick, and Arin Sang-urai.

Thank you, Donica Bettanin, for taking our show to the Ubud Writers and Readers Festival. Thank you to Helen Withycombe and Michael Williams for inviting us to celebrate immigration at the Wheeler Centre in Melbourne.

Thanks to friends of *Alien Nation*, including Mazin Sidahmed and Max Siegelbaum at *Documented*; Arielle Kandel and the New Women New Yorkers; Mark Nowak and the Worker Writers School; Onassis Democracy Festival; The Moth. Thank you, Libby Flores, Johanna Castillo, and Jenelle Pifer.

Thanks to the Flatiron Page Turners, and to my students at Catapult for inspiration. Thanks to Adi Diner for the word. Thanks to my dear friends and sounding boards Abeer Hoque, Angela Ledgerwood, Bojana Novakovic, Estelle Tang, and Xochitl Gonzalez. This book came together during a tough year—thanks to those who were here: Julia Solomon, Betsy

Hegeman, the families of Brontë, Cyrus, Gregory, Izzy, and Stewart.

Stojanka and Natalija Stefanovic, I am grateful for your love and support, no matter how far you are. Michael Hart and Leon, I am grateful for your love and support, no matter how close you are.

Credits and Permissions

About the Author

SOFIJA STEFANOVIC is the creator and host of This Alien Nation, a celebration of immigration. Her memoir, *Miss Ex-Yugoslavia*, is a sometimes funny, sometimes dark, story about being an immigrant kid during the Yugoslavian Wars. She's a regular storyteller with The Moth and has traveled with their Mainstage telling personal stories across the country. Her writing has appeared in publications such as the *New York Times*, among others.

A Note from the Cover Designer

Being an immigrant has let me connect to my neighbors across the street and to struggles across the world, more so than any socioeconomic, racial, or political designation. As an immigrant from a line of immigrants, growing up and building a life among immigrants, I've found community in a constellation of shared experiences simultaneously universal and specific.

The live show This Alien Nation created a rare space for audiences to devote attention to each distinctive voice. Whether stepping into the spotlight or listening from the crowd, the space would grow with each story shared. Estranged parts of ourselves felt familiar again as we were reacquainted with these experiences that we too rarely hear and explore outside the theater doors. An infectious invitation would ripple through the room as emboldened strangers would lean between tables, the lobby bubbling with the audience and performers switching places. After an hour attentively listening in the dark together, it was impossible to set out into the street without feeling changed, closer to one another, and keenly aware of all our connections. This is represented in my drawing as a speaker steps forward to stand alone in the spotlight—but they have the support of a larger community of immigrants behind them with their own stories ready to be heard.

—Matt Huynh

Here ends Sofija Stefanovic's
Alien Nation.

The first edition of this book was printed and
bound at LSC Communications in
Harrisonburg, Virginia, September 2021.

A NOTE ON THE TYPE

The text of this book was set in Bembo, a serif typeface based
on the work of Francesco Griffo, who originally cut the
type at the end of the fifteenth century for use by Venetian
printer Aldus Manutius. The typeface, which departed from
the common pen-drawn calligraphy of the day and influenced typefaces like Garamond and Times Roman, is named
for Pietro Bembo, the Venetian poet, cardinal, and literary theorist active through the sixteenth century. In 1929,
Stanley Morison of Monotype revived and expanded this
classical yet readable typeface to adapt to the machine composition and typesetting requirements of the day. Monotype
released a digital version in 2005.

HARPERVIA

An imprint dedicated to publishing international voices,
offering readers a chance to encounter other lives and other
points of view via the language of the imagination.